CHICAGO'S GODS:

THE MAFIA MEETS BHAGAVAD GITA

ANDREW A. KENNY

Also by Andrew A. Kenny:

Easy and Natural:
Sex, Jail, Yoga and Chili, 2011

God, Angels, Yoga and Maslow:
A Search for Meaning in a Chaotic World, 2013

DEDICATIONS:

The Theosophical Advaita Vedanta Study Group, Wheaton, IL, where they consider the significant issues about the oneness of all life open to discussion.

Elizabeth Kubler Ross: *Death and Dying*

Sri Nisargadatta Maharaj: *I Am*

Rupert Spira: *The Transparency of Things*

Chip Hartranft: The *Yoga Sutra* of Patanjali, a Shambhala Classic

The Uribe Family: Joel Senior, Claudia and Joel Junior who, someday, will know his luck being born into a family with good hearts.

TABLE OF CONTENTS

INTRODUCTION:

There are a few difficulties with language in what is written here:

- Language is knowledge of the mind, conceptual in nature and because of that it is divorced from existence.

- Language cannot adequately describe anything, in particular action or experience of the senses. We depend on social agreement to make language work.

- Therefore the language in this book is my best attempt to provide access to knowledge of the ineffable.

There are four main characters in this book:

- Amos-A shell shocked veteran of WWII. He is considering going to heroin for his problems, but he knows this would be a problem. In the meanwhile he is drinking muscatel with Mike. The Don expects Amos to work for him because he helped his family while Amos was away in the war. He is twenty four years old.

- Andy-An avid reader, he picked up a copy of the Bhagavad Gita recommended by an alcoholic priest when he was an altar boy at Holy Family grammar school and started to take religion seriously. He's studied it but is having trouble understanding it. He has avoided life by reading and by the religion's injunction to be "humble." He is only eighteen years old, but grew up with Amos before the war.

- Mike DeBarlo-A fruit and vegetable peddler that operates from the back of his horse and wagon. He grew up in poverty and hunger; his parents died when he was young, the mafia Don bought him a horse and wagon so he could distribute heroin while selling fruits and vegetables. He moves the raw heroin that he picks up at the South Water Market to those that cut and bag it. He supplies the heroin in bags to the dealers where he picks up the money for the Don, Vittorio Calabrese at the end of each day. He tells the stories of the day to the Don. He also carries a pint of Muscatel wine at all times that he uses to medicate his anxiety. He has a photographic memory letting him give the Don an accurate description of the day's events. He is forty five years old.

- The three friends: Mike DeBarlo, Amos and Andy drive around the neighborhood selling fruits and vegetables, and talking about Amos's problems and their lives. Their route every day takes them from the horse and wagon barn on Loomis between Roosevelt and Grenshaw to the South Water Market on Racine to buy the day's fruits and vegetables and back through the Chicago streets and housing projects selling his produce and moving bulk heroin on the way. Andy, the intellectual, brings a copy of the Bhagavad Gita he has read, but has not understood. He has outlined some questions and thinks that it will do his old friend, Amos, some good if they all discuss the questions since it is about a warrior that has lost his nerve. At his mother's prompting he decides to form an informal Theosophical Study Group.

- Vittorio Calabrese, the Don-A mafia leader distributing heroin, a new opportunity after WWII. He also runs the bathroom towel small business shakedown racket and controls the Chicago juke box plays along with his connections in Hollywood. He doesn't like to go outside unless he has business to do-then he gets purposeful. He is a graduate of Saint Ignatius High School. He thinks he is protected from the drug laws because of the help given Army Intelligence during the war by the mafia. He believes having a strong culture like the Mafia and being Italian is very important in life. He helped out Amos' family during the war. He expects Amos to pay him back by working as an enforcer for him. He is sixty years old.

CHAPTER ONE:

WHEN TROUBLE COMES, AWARENESS RISES. (DENIAL)

Foreword: Andy asks Mike to take Amos and him around the neighborhood to see how the drug trade has affected things. Amos is worried and curious about his friends and neighbors who he knows are involved as users and dealers. He is also concerned because he is unable to work because of shell shock from being in the army in Europe. He has been tempted to try some heroin "just to calm down," or at least relieve his anxiety. Andy brings a copy of the Gita. At the end of the first day, Mike tells the Don what they talked about.

MIKE

Hey Vittorio, here are your potatoes; (the money collections for the day are hidden in the potatoes. The heroin from the South Water market is hidden in the baskets of potatoes to start and distributed to the dealers as the horse and wagon moves around the area selling fruits and vegetables.); it's all there. I spent the day on the wagon with a couple of guys from the neighborhood. Don't worry; they don't know what's happening. I figure the cover is better with three of us. We're going to go out every day and talk about an old book about life and good and bad and all that stuff: The Bhagavad Gita. I'll keep you informed how each day went. Andy usually

I

makes a statement or asks a question from the Bhagavad Gita that we then discuss. Here's what was said on the first day:

VITTORIO

Keep me up to date on your discussions. I had a priest that used to quote the Gita many years ago in Italy, when I was in grammar school. I never forgot the priest using a Holy Book from another religion. I was impressed but I never did come to believe that Hindu stuff. Here's a little something for your help. Let me know what each of you said during the day.

MIKE

I'll start each comment with the name of who's speaking:

ANDY

Hey Mike; how about taking Amos and me with you on your rounds? Amos is having trouble. He jumps a mile every time he hears a noise and sometimes any kind of funny sound. He needs to get around and see what's happening in the old neighborhood. He needs some help getting back into life.

MIKE

Climb up guys. This horse can pull a couple extra bodies. You can help sell some of the sweet corn. Just yell out "sweet corn, gotcha sweet corn" at each stop. What's the book, Andy?

ANDY

I brought a copy of an old book about a war where the hero got help from God when he lost his nerve. I was going to go over it with Amos to see if it would click and maybe help him with his fears. I read it, but don't really understand it. I don't even know why I have so much trouble with it. You guys have a lot more experience in the world, maybe you can help me? I made a list of questions from each chapter.

MIKE

OK. Give us the questions, one at a time, and we'll kick them around. I'll make a few notes for the Don; he's very interested in this stuff. He heard about it back in Italy.

ANDY

The first one is **what runs the mind to control the body?** I know that if I'm drunk, for instance, I act different from when I'm sober; it's common to fall down or have mood swings, for instance.

AMOS

When you hear bombs exploding all around you, and you piss your pants or worse, the noise has changed your actions. But, then your training kicks in and you start shooting as the enemy comes at you. So, your experience counts for something as well. But a lot of the guys hid in their foxholes and even their training didn't help. Of course, they were worn out from all the killing they had seen or done.

MIKE

I can relate to getting drunk. The same thing holds if you're high on heroin. Or, if you're holding some drugs, or a gun, and the police drive by, it's all you can do to act normal, when you really want to run down the alley.

GOOD AND BAD:

ANDY

OK. The second question is **what is good and what is bad**? If you're hungry and steal a candy bar, is that bad? If you skip mass on Sunday, is it a sin, even if you're not Catholic? Is always being good the only way to live?

AMOS

I think that war is bad. All those people getting slaughtered. Think about the bombing that kills thousands at a time. Good is not going to war in the first place. The Catholics are not the only good people out here. I have plenty of Jewish friends who I trust with my life.

MIKE

This is more complicated than we think. I know some priests that I don't trust. They get too close to the young boys and women in the parish. And, sometimes we have to go to war because we are fighting for the good, or against a dictator. The good must involve leaders that have good hearts, and know what they are doing, providing education and good jobs for the people to make our society a better place to live. Even the mafia has some good characteristics. Their culture goes back longer than the beginning of America.

ANDY

The third question is **how do we move towards the good**? (See chapter 19) It seems to me that it can only be done by individuals. Or maybe someone that has a lot of power could do something that will be good for a lot of people. Give them all a copy of the Gita or provide food for the poor. It's kind of like putting chlorine in the water: it benefits everyone.

AMOS

I'm still not sure that the war had any good in it. Maybe the soldiers that hid in their foxholes did good because they didn't shoot anyone, even though it was their duty. I suppose that doing good has to do with doing your duty, even when you don't want to. Since I've left the army I don't know what my duty is; I feel lost. And now that I'm home, I see that my old friends and family are involved with heroin. I can see how it's tempting. My old crush, Dorothy, has become a prostitute to get money for drugs. This stuff is destroying the neighborhood. It's pretty depressing. I don't know what to do.

MIKE

Most of the neighborhood is involved with drugs. I think it's beyond us. Maybe this Gita will help us to see what can be done. It's deep stuff. I haven't thought about these things since I went on a retreat in grammar school. You guys know that I work for the Don. I sometimes wonder if I am going to go to hell for it. I don't feel like I'm doing anything wrong. If it wasn't me it would be someone else. I grew up in the business; I'll live in the business; and I'll die in the business; it's all I know how to do; I'm Italian.

ANDY

Well, maybe the next question will steer us a little: **Is there good in bad and bad in good?** I know that the war was hell for those that were over there, but it did do some good for those countries over there, didn't it?

AMOS

Those countries and a lot of their population were destroyed, but I guess we are going to help them rebuild with the Marshall Plan. Perhaps there is some good for the future generations. That's what's meant by some good in the bad. What could some bad in the good be? Perhaps those priests that are getting too close to young boys and girls are an example of some bad in good.

MIKE

For me the Mafia is an example of good in bad. Most of the guys are good family men and support their church and lead good lives except for their part in the mafia, and most of that isn't really bad. Moving drugs or money around isn't bad in itself; it's only in the long run that you can see some bad. In fact, now that I'm thinking about this, we don't ever think about the effect of some sin for the long run; we can't predict the outcome of any of our actions. If we kill a bad guy that could be a good thing because if a bad guy has a long life, he could do a lot of harm to others. But how do we judge our actions?

DIRECTION IN LIFE:

ANDY

OK. The next question is **if there is a good way to be, how do we make sure that we always move in the right direction**? I think that we all know, in our hearts, what to do that is right. We have a conscience that tells us. Otherwise we would be automatically following a bunch or rules someone wrote a long time ago. And there are always exceptions to rules. Language is not always enough to describe correct actions; it can't accurately describe experiences or actions. And, it is not always the action we do that's important, but what motivates the action. We need to have good hearts, because we don't always know our own motivations, let alone the motivations of others. It's has a lot to do with the way we are brought up, our family, our culture. In America we have a lot of different cultures, so we get mixed messages. Consider the Ten Commandments' with some obvious exceptions:

	Commandment	Comments
1.	I am the LORD your God: you shall not have strange Gods before me.	All Gods are strange. We don't know anything about them. Does this mean there are other Gods?
2.	You shall not take the name of the LORD your God in vain.	Everyone is always saying god damn it or Jesus Christ! Is this one of the worst sins we can think of? Are these the top ten?
3.	Remember to keep holy the LORD'S Day.	Every religion turns this into a sin. If we don't go to church they don't make money.

4.	Honor your father and your mother.	What if your father beats the kids and mother? What if the mother is sleeping around?
5.	You shall not kill.	Except when the priests send us to war, or if you are a cop, and many other excuses. What about if you step on an ant, or kill a cow or chicken?
6.	You shall not commit adultery.	Good luck with all the women's husbands away in the army
7.	You shall not steal.	Stealing is part of our lives here. What can you do when you're hungry, even starving or need drugs?
8.	You shall not bear false witness against your neighbor.	We don't tell the cops anything, especially about our friends.
9.	You shall not covet your neighbor's wife.	Covet means wanting. The way some of the neighbor's wives dress, how can we help it. It's automatic.
10.	You shall not covet your neighbor's goods.	When you are poor and don't have enough to eat, you can't help wanting some of the neighbor's spaghetti. Sometimes I wish I had good shoes in the winter.

These are not the worst sins we can think of. They are only some of the rules that some religions teach. These mortal sins are nothing compared to dropping an atomic bomb on a city and killing a couple hundred thousand, or sending our army into some foreign country and killing their people just to feed the war industries. Or, what about, the tricks some businesses use to cheat their customers and employees? We need commandments for Governments and business, don't you think?

AMOS

Hey Mike, pay attention, you have a customer back of the wagon; Rosa wants some sweet corn. Hey Rosa, how do you be good?

ROSA

When I'm good I shake it all around. You remember me don't you Amos?

AMOS

It's been a long time Rosa. Glad to see you now. I just got back a few weeks ago. I'll see you around.

Hey Andy, does the good apply to sex also? You know, sometimes sex is good and sometimes you wish you were somewhere else.

ANXIETY:

ANDY

We're talking about being good as applying to every part of life. It seems almost impossible, because our minds don't seem to be under control all the time. I can't even stop thinking when I go to sleep at night. It takes a long time to fall asleep. I even had to learn a relaxation procedure from a book *HOW TO STOP WORRYING AND START LIVING* by Dale Carnegie.

The next question is **what should we do to prepare**? Is there some way to live so that we will always do what's right?

AMOS

I don't see how we can be ready for all the things that come up. We hardly ever know what will come up next. It's like a roll of the dice. We just do our best as life happens to us. We don't even know what thoughts we will think, or how we will feel five minutes from now. But the war taught me that we can at least try to avoid doing harm to someone in everyday life. But what if someone tries to hold you up and you have a gun? Do you shoot them to protect what you own?

MIKE

There's no question in my mind. Pull the gun out and do what you have to do. Maybe the guy was under the influence. How do you fix the guy so he don't do some harm to the next victim? He has to, at least, get a beating.

TRADITIONS:

ANDY

The next question is **are family traditions or culture important**? I'm Irish and I can see big differences in the way we talk and the foods we eat between my family, the Jewish families, the Italian families, and their cultures as well. Is one culture better than another? My Father and his brothers were all big drinkers, but they also held intelligence very important, testing me with riddles every time we got together for a family party or picnic.

AMOS

After being in the war, I was hungry to be home, in the neighborhood, with my friends. It's hard to explain, even to myself, how important all this is. It's a big relief, just to be here, but I'm anxious at the same time. I don't know if it's the culture, the neighborhood, or what, but it's an important even sacred part of our lives.

MIKE

My family was all destroyed by the depression. I made a living selling fruits and vegetables from the South Water Market. I was helped by the Mafia and now I'm OK. I still sleep in the barn, and have to take care of my horse and wagon, but at least I own my own business. If I'm in a culture, it's the American culture. I sell in a lot of different areas, the projects are mixed; Taylor Street is mostly Italian; 18th Street is polish; and there are all the black neighborhoods near hear. I fit in with all of them. They all like sweet corn, apples, peaches and strawberries.

ANDY

The last question of the day is **can families and individuals improve spiritually**? My mother, for instance, is a member of the Rosicrucian Society and practices meditation which is said to help us advance spiritually. They talk about it as overcoming our ignorance of reality. She is the one that let me have a copy of the Gita; it was printed by the Theosophical Society. They have their main headquarters out west in Wheaton.

AMOS

I'm not sure about spirituality in the family, but you see a lot of it in the fox holes when the bombs are going off. The war as a whole leaves a lot of worn out men that don't think about god except when they are in immediate danger, begging him to save them. I don't think we know much about God or our Souls. In the Catholic Churches that I've gone to there were a lot of statues and pictures, but they don't mean anything. Even the bible says don't put false idols before me. Those statues, pictures and stained glass windows in the church are not the real thing, they're just decorations.

MIKE

I've thought a lot about that idea when my mother committed suicide and my father drank his self to death. I was just a little kid and then grew up with my aunt and uncle. They were pretty poor, so I only had what I could steal. I didn't even think about stealing being wrong. When I see other poor kids stealing a candy bar or even a tomato from the Water Market stands it don't seem wrong to me. If you're hungry and you steel to feed your body, that's spiritual to me.

VITTORIO

Hey, don't forget to bring me the story each day. This is the kind of stuff the mafia has had historical interest in, especially the bad in good and the good in bad. I hope studying the Gita will be good for Amos's problems.

I **don't believe** in that Hindu stuff, myself; the bible is good enough for me. Hey, tell Amos to come and see me. I helped his family out during the war while he was away. He owes me.

You think Amos has problems; try growing up in a mafia family; your relatives getting arrested; having to kill someone you don't even know.

Amos thinks the war was a bad news. It don't amount to much when you consider that 100,000,000 people die each year from natural causes, 21,000,000 or more of those die from hunger, 3,000,000 of the deaths from hunger are children. The mafia has always kept death in context.

Bring Amos in to see me next time. I know just what he needs to straighten him out.

CHAPTER TWO:

WHEN TROUBLE COMES, AND IT ALWAYS COMES, LOOK FOR FRIENDS TO HELP.

Foreword: After asking Mike to pick them up each day the three of them agree to study the Gita.

MIKE

Hey Vittorio, there are no potatoes today. The shipment was late getting into the market. I was able to move some bags to the dealers on Laughlin Street so the business is still going good. No complaints from the street. There's a new cop named "Brown" that is assigned strictly to narcotics. He seems to be concentrating on the users for now. We did spend a day getting into the second chapter of the Gita. I'm getting to like this discussion and the way it's going. The three of us are good cover, but some of the dealers are asking questions. Here's what we talked about on the second day:

DON

Just keep me informed, Mike. What you told me got me thinking as well. I especially like the part about not being able to know good from bad. I can see how confusion can come up when no one can know the long term effects of any of our actions. Even little changes can multiply over long times and who knows what the effect might be? I think that staying with your culture or family teaches you how to act and that has to be the best guideline. Otherwise we are all lost.

MIKE

On the second day the ideas were harder to understand.

THE CHANGING SELF:

ANDY

One of the main parts of the Gita has to do with what a human being is. **Why do we think we are the same self when we are always changing? Are we the body or a soul? What is a soul?** First we are born, spend some time as a baby, gradually grow up, get older and then die. Our bodies change every day, and we learn new things all the time, both on the street and in school. So our bodies and minds and even our feelings are constantly changing. But, somehow we always seem to be the same. Why?

The Gita also says: That which is not, shall never be; that which is, shall never cease to be. To the wise, these truths are self-evident. To me this means that whatever part of us is changing is not real; that points to our bodies and minds. It is a truth about existence. Things that come and go are empty of inherent existence, as the Buddhists say. Everything that we perceive is like a wave, it all appears and then disappears. The "knower," the "perceiver" never changes.

AMOS

Even during the fighting in the war, sometimes when I could see who I was shooting at it seemed like I was looking at myself. We are all the same in some mystical way that we don't understand. But, still, the war had an effect on me, but I don't feel any different than when I was a kid; I never felt OK then either. I'm still the person who knows what's going on in my life.

MIKE

I feel the same. I'm the same person looking out now that I was when I was a hungry thief. And, the stealing didn't change me in any way that I know about. I'm smarter now, and probably wiser, but that don't change what I am.

Hey Amos, Vittorio wants to see you. He has some work for you. You know that he helped your family when you were in the war; now it's time for payback.

ANDY

Well that brings us to the second question: **Is there a soul?** Do we have a soul or does the soul have us? It don't seem like it is anything we can know about. The Church says we have one and it will go to heaven, hell or purgatory, depending how we act while we are here. Their rules seem a little authoritarian to me. Do we have a soul, or does the soul have us?

AMOS

It's a good question. Even during the worst fighting, when I thought I was sure to die, it was still the same me watching it all. The watching part seems like it hasn't changed during my whole life. Maybe that's the soul? We can't watch the watcher or know the knower.

MIKE

I think you're onto something, Amos. The soul has to relate to our lives in some way. If it's watching it all, that's about as close as it can get. It sees it all, watches our thoughts, feels our feelings, and tastes the food we eat, listens to the music and enjoys it all. To the soul, it seems like a movie or a play, except it is more realistic. It is real life. I wonder if it can cause us to act a certain way.

THE BODY:

ANDY

Well if we are really a soul, looking at life, **does it matter what happens to the body?** I know a lot of things matter to me, but I'm not sure about the "watcher." If the body dies at a young age, the soul doesn't get its money worth out of life. Does it then go to heaven? The church says the soul of a baby goes to purgatory. What is heaven really like?

AMOS

I saw a lot of death in the war. I don't like to think of a soul paying attention to its body being torn apart by bombs, or dying slowly after being shot. When something hurts us does it hurt the soul?

MIKE

I don't think my soul watches my thoughts. I've had some wild thoughts in my time. The watcher never said anything about any of it. Doesn't it care? If the body does bad things does the soul hurt? If the soul is not involved why don't it go to heaven no matter what happens? The soul is not doing anything, is it? I don't think we have this all figured out.

WISDOM:

ANDY

What do the realized people say? This stuff has been studied for thousands of years and many experts have made comments about it. Most of them say that we are confused or ignorant about what this life is all about. They describe what we are by using a capital S for the true Self. I think, by that, they mean something like what we are talking about as the soul. They sometimes call it the witness. As we grow up our ego develops and takes over our life. Habits are formed and we are at the mercy of them; we don't know they are habits. We become automations, avoiding things we don't like and trying to get things we want. There are all kinds of ways to break through this "illusion" to get free of our conditioning. The Sufi's say **if you want to break out of jail, you must first realize that you are in jail.** This means that we need to break the ego cage of "I," "me," and "mine," which is all conditioning. The Buddhist all say a first step is to look for the "I" and when you realize that it doesn't exist you have made the first step to knowing reality.

AMOS

Well this life doesn't seem like an illusion. But when I was in England I went to a Shakespeare play where one of the lines was – this life is but a play and we are just players on the stage. I think that he had the same idea. This play of life must be for the Self, our soul.

MIKE

What about my horse? Does she have a soul, or watcher, or Self, whatever word we use. I just realized that language is not able to accurately describe what we are talking about. I know that doesn't mean that we can't understand it. Even horses understand things. Language isn't up to describing any experience, let alone the ineffable, such as God or the Soul.

REINCARNATION:

ANDY

Another question: **is reincarnation what happens after death?** My mother's books all describe reincarnation as the truth. I don't know how this affects the Catholic idea of heaven and hell forever. I can see how life on earth can be heaven or hell, depending on your luck. Another idea from the Gita is: **The soul was not born; it will never die; it is Unborn, Eternal, and Ever-enduring; it does not die when the body dies; it experiences infancy, youth and old age.**

AMOS

I'm guessing that the next life depends on what we do in this life. But if we are automatons, at the mercy of our conditioning, how can we be blamed for what we do? Is this whole world on automatic pilot? If we can break out of our conditioning, do we get out of reincarnation? What do I do about being depressed?

I don't know if I can believe this stuff.

MIKE

I must have screwed up a lot in my past life to get what happened to me in this life: hungry kid, parents die early, barely get through grammar school, working at the South Water Market packing tomatoes until Vittorio bought me this horse and wagon so I could make some money.

CONDITIONING:

ANDY

All the great experts say **we should break the bonds of our conditioning**. There are all kinds of suggestions about how to do this: avoid attachments, watch your motivations, beware the mind for it is exceedingly wicked, do your work without expectations, practice selfless service to others, study good books, find a teacher, use your intuition, and practice meditation. And Amos, in your case the Gita has a special message: **Do not yield to fear or depression. Shake it off and do what you should. Also, consciousness**, which pervades all that we see, is imperishable. There is no need to worry or be depressed about anything.

AMOS

I can kind of see how we are conditioned. When I joined the army I had to learn a new living routine. I had a lot of habits that I had to break, like waking up late and eating whenever I felt like cooking, or had money for a hot dog. And then I had to learn new habits, like dressing a certain way, and making my bed just right. It was kind of a shock until I picked up the new stuff. But, now, I see that I just replaced my old conditioning and habits with new ones. Maybe that's all we ever do. How do I break the bonds of my depression? Alcohol seems to help a little, but it's hard to control. Would heroin work better? If I have to wait for my depression and anxiety to leave before I get a job, I'll never work. I'll have to get a job where I'm not supervised much. Maybe I'll get the GI bill and go to college.

MIKE

I I know that I have a lot of habits, mostly bad. I could probably break most of them, but I would be pretty anxious. I need a few beers at night or I don't sleep well. I enjoy playing pool on days when I'm not working; why should I give up everything I like? I'd really have to believe this stuff to quit all my bad habits.

TROUBLE:

ANDY

The way we get into trouble follows a path: we form attachment to sense objects (things we like); desire builds and habituation turns to lust; when we can't get what we want we get angry; and anger affects our judgment which screws up our life. When our life is wasted there is no peace or joy. I remember I had a crush on Dorothy and she got hooked on drugs and started selling herself. I was really mad about it. So I reacted by going out with a married women. That was not right. I made a bad choice. I had to climb out a third floor window when her husband came home one morning. I'm lucky I didn't die.

AMOS

When I came back to America after being in the war a long time, I felt kind of loose. It's like I don't have any strong attachments except that I react strongly to noises. I'm floating around with you guys on this wagon. It's pleasant. I don't even want a beer, but I enjoy a little of Mike's muscatel once in a while.

MIKE

I guess I don't see my attachments as that strong an influence. I drink a few beers at night, and I see some of the old winos so I know what could happen, but I doubt that it'll happen to me. Maybe we're only talking about strong attachments, like heroin addiction. Those guys will steal from their friends and families and do anything just to get high.

STIMULUS-RESPONSE:

ANDY

I think what the Gita is getting at is that **our lives are all in a reaction mode; it is all based on stimulus-response; we've been conditioned; it's like using treats to train a dog. This is considered part of the illusion (maya) that is part of our misunderstanding of how the world works.** We all think we are in control of something we call "our life." It doesn't happen in a vacuum: the rest of the world has to be exactly as it is to allow us "our" life.

AMOS

You mean that my being relaxed now is part of my reaction to being in the war? I can see that. If someone started shooting I would change instantly. This has already happened when a car backfired the other day. I dropped to the ground and tried to hide. That's my idea of stimulus-response: I'm relaxed, something happens, I hide, and my depression returns.

MIKE

What I know about this is that if I signal my horse to turn, she turns, if I signal her to stop, she stops. If you want me to do something I ask how much you will pay me. If I drink too much I'll have a hangover. But there's something more: I have already planned for the fact that I need money to support myself. I have already bought food for the horse. There are a thousand things we do for ourselves without really thinking about it. We automatically watch out when crossing the street. I just got it: we have already organized our lives to avoid the things that we don't want and made plans to get the things we want; it is already done. Another way of saying it is that we are done for. Of course, we can think and act on purpose, but we know how difficult it is to control our minds; if we can't control our minds what does that tell us about our actions? We are under automatic control by the mind that has been programmed by a baby: one of our favorite pastimes is sucking tits.

SINS:

ANDY

How do we know the right thing to do? If we are all on automatic pilot, how do we know that what we are doing is the right thing? How do we make real choices? What are real alternatives? When you're hungry and stealing candy bars the only point of reference is the nuns have told us that stealing is a sin. You like candy or maybe the feeling of excitement so you do it anyway. I don't know if stimulus-response has anything to do with right and wrong. But if you're stuck in acting this way how can you be blamed for any "sins" you commit?

AMOS

It seems like you're saying that there is nothing really wrong with war or killing or drug addiction or any of this. It's just the world doing its thing. That's far out man. It like do what you do and **relax**. That seems too easy. I got it. Even if we relax, we will still run into things that make us unhappy. My depression comes back. It's just the way the world works. I don't see how you can just get rid of depression.

MIKE

I got it. If you eat, you shit. It's automatic. What you think of shit has nothing to do with it. Our thoughts just come and go based on prior conditioning. The mind just keeps throwing up explanations and justifications that may or may not be accurate. It's just doing its thing. Language is never up to the job of adequate explanation of life.

IMPROVEMENTS:

ANDY

It's not that simple. **Once you have heard about this stuff, your job is to work to recognize and change your conditioning, for the better. You should make this a major commitment in your life.** We should make an effort, no matter how little. Religious experts normally don't help, at least the priests that we know. I have to make an exception for the priest that passed on the Gita. They are usually just selling their own brand of ideology that has been passed down to them. They are as conditioned as we are. But, we all need conditioning and habits: we couldn't walk without it. 54r

AMOS

I hear you. When I was in the war I just reacted like I was trained. There's nothing wrong with that. Doing the things that you are trained to do is ok. But now, when we see how all this is misleading, and that we are on automatic pilot and don't know it, our job is to find out how we and others are stuck in our circumstances. I think I can see it. Our job is to learn how to change, without all the stress and complaints.

MIKE

I'm starting to see it too. I can see that my horse does what I have trained her to do. But, you could say that she has trained me to give her the right signals. We are all training each other starting at birth, through school and the rest of life. We don't even understand cause and effect. For anything to happen there has to be an infinite number of preceding supporting causes as well as an absence of causes that would have prevented the result.

DUALITY:

ANDY

For a start **they say that we should give up the confusion caused by the sense of duality: me/them, good/bad, and pain/pleasure. We should free ourselves from desire and avoidance to find peace.** I think, by peace, they mean that we now know what's actually happening in life, and we are satisfied that we are on the right track. By "giving up" is meant that we reach the point of acceptance where we are comfortable in the change the knowledge brings to us.

AMOS

Well if we have another war, I'm going to avoid it no matter what these teachings say. I just realized, I don't really know what I would do if another war came along. That was just my mind pushing a thought. I do that a lot.

MIKE

I know what you mean. For example, Andy is always making other people wrong in order to make himself right. It's easy for me to see, but for him it is automatic. I don't think of right and wrong for other people. We each judge ourselves so much we don't need anyone to add to it. I know I grew up in poverty, with all its disadvantages, and that affected me in a lot of ways. I pinch pennies when I go to buy anything. I deny myself little things that I probably could afford. I don't think that I could give up the idea of me against them. Maybe it means the golden rule: "do unto others as you would they do unto you?"

Hey Amos, come with me to Vittorio's when we're done here. He wants to see you.

VITTORIO

That's important stuff, Mike. Especially about all of us being conditioned and not free to do what may be right. That means there is no such thing as sin, unless you are free. This is also a teaching of the Mafia. When you are ordered to go and kill someone that you don't know, eventually you realize that you are just part of a larger organization doing your work. Some can't handle it and they live in guilt that ruins their lives. I'm beginning to think that this Hindu stuff may be OK.

When you get beyond guilt; you know it don't depend on you; you just do what's necessary; you're a "made" man. We all are subject to conditioning that is overcome through selfless service. The Mafia is all about service. We are the political alternative.

Now Amos, I have a little work for you. There's a tavern on Taylor and Loomis that is playing stuff on the juke box that I haven't agreed to. I want you to go straighten him out. Don't explain anything to him. Just go in with a baseball bat and break up the juke box and leave. If he hollers or tries anything, use the bat on him. Here, use this bat. I bought it special for the occasion.

CHAPTER THREE:

WHEN WE INCREASE CONSCIOUSNESS WE OBSERVE MORE PROBLEMS, FOR OURSELVES AND FOR OTHERS. WITH CLARITY ABOUT LIFE, THE DIRECTION OF EVOLUTION CAN BE CHANGED FOR THE BETTER BY CHANGING YOURSELF. RIGHT ACTION CHANGES THE FUTURE FOR THE GOOD.

Foreword: They discuss doing their duty without attachment to results.

MIKE

Hey Vittorio, we got two bushels of potatoes today. Business must be good. We are getting into a lot of deep stuff in our discussions:

DON

I'm really enjoying your reports, Mike. We are all raised up by parents that, in my case, were part of a strong culture. I feel very much that I'm a product of my conditioning. I don't fight it. I don't see why we should try to fight it. I need to hear more about this stuff, especially about the soul, the inner self.

MIKE

. Here's what we talked about on the third day:

WORK ON THE PATH:

ANDY

Two actions we can take to free ourselves are: **selfless service is the first; contemplation of the wisdom presented in the Gita is the second.** I see selfless service as helping out in life, especially when it something we don't want to do, like, for me, cleaning the toilet at home when it's dirty. I have also contemplated being right by making others wrong. It was a revelation. I've been keeping my mind to myself since then. I shut off the external speaker.

AMOS

I think that being in the war was selfless service. I didn't want to be there. I see something: **Selfless service means making a choice.** I didn't make a choice to go to war; I was drafted. When I clean up the pool room at night because Kaiser is too tired, that's selfless service. When I was in the war I thought a lot about war; I think it is wrong. It is always very complicated; politicians often justify it; their friends make money.

At the end of the day drop me off by the tavern on Taylor and Loomis. I have some work to do for Vittorio.

MIKE

For me, selfless service means taking care of my horse and wagon-no, I see now that's just doing my duty. Selfless service is when I give some of the poor women a little extra when they are buying vegetables, or give the kids a few strawberries or a piece of watermelon. But, that may be questionable because when I do that it makes me feel good. Driving around with a horse and wagon all day gives me plenty of time to think about life. I guess I do a lot more thinking now; I have something to really think about.

COMPASSION:

ANDY

Hey Mike, what you are doing when you give some of your produce to the poor is **being compassionate.** You have a good heart, and that is an important part of this work. For many people, their desires prevent them from being compassionate.

AMOS

After the war, in Europe, we supplied the people with food, medicine and clothes. A lot of places were bombed out and they didn't have anything. I guess you could say that America was being compassionate. I passed out quite a few candy bars myself; compassion was in the air there.

MIKE

Selfless service and compassion go hand-in-hand. The feeling that I get when I give away food to someone that needs it must be compassion. I like that feeling and plan to keep doing that stuff no matter how I feel about the individuals. I guess I could even go out of my way to help others that need help. I don't seem to do it that way. It seems automatic to me, and that's OK.

TWO PATHS:

ANDY

The Gita says that **all this, including whatever we consider our-selves to be, the mind and body, are part of nature. We are all conditioned, and operate automatically. There is no single oper-ator in life, no single cause that can be identified.** I don't know how all of us studying the Gita fit into this "automatic" description. I know what the words mean, but I don't really understand it. I think some kind of expe-rience is needed, or some kind of acceptance is necessary. My mind doesn't want to go there. There are two paths: the first is the path of contemplation and meditation and the second is the Path of Action for those who perform selfless service. Even though we are conditioned and our bodies are part of nature, right action should be our intention; we should plan for it.

AMOS

If all this is part of nature, then war and all the sins we know about don't mean anything. I can almost see it. When I was in the middle of war, I didn't plan my actions, I just did them whether I was fighting or hiding. No one had to teach me to duck when bombs were going off, or shoot when the enemy was com-ing. I didn't have to forgive myself for shooting someone, and I didn't think of it as a sin. It was all just happening. My thoughts were just happening as well.

MIKE

If we are all just part of nature, then we are not much different from my horse. I know that she is part of nature, but we have the ability to think and solve problems. There must be some order in nature. Say plants to trees, or bugs to animals to birds, or monkeys to apes to man. By our measure we are high in the order of things. But, I can see that being high on the list doesn't mean we are beyond nature. We are still part of it. I get it.

LIFE OPERATIONS:

ANDY

I think you're right. The Gita explains that **the Self operates the intellect, the intellect leads the mind, the mind leads the senses, and the senses lead the body. Its advice is to let the Self rule the ego (habitual fears and desires) to rid the self of selfish desires.** This way of talking about the Self with a capital "S" is difficult to understand. Taking the advice makes us aware of the distinction between this higher self and nature. Nature operates with attraction and repulsion, like gravity or magnetism. When we witness this operation in our built in laboratory we become more and more aware of the Self as not being part of this field. Normally, we are motivated by what we want and don't want. When we resist and become aware of this we start to move towards freedom.

AMOS

It's like when the enemy was coming at us and at some point we didn't hide or run, but just stood up and kept shooting. Nothing meant anything anymore except doing the job. Up until that point we were motivated by trying to save ourselves and get comfortable. It's like two different operating techniques. But now I'm stuck in something. They call it shell shock. But, even so, I am able to resist it slightly, and sometimes even observe the sensations and relax. There is no doubt in my mind that this is an automatic part of being human. The example is extreme, but accurate.

MIKE

It's like the mind has a map of where I want to go. I look around with my senses and memory of the map and move and turn the horse when necessary. The horse may prefer to go back to the barn, but it follows my direction. Selfish desires are not obviously involved. They do come up when I feel the need to go to the bathroom, for instance. Sometimes I have to go two or three hours before I find the opportunity. It's a strong desire, but I can resist it.

VITTORIO

My boys and I do the collection for the church; the money is good; when they don't have money for the basket; we pull them out of the pew; they can get the same benefit by standing in the back.

Americans donate over $250,000,000,000 each year to churches and charities. Religion is a good racket. I wonder how much the Hindus make off this stuff.

Hey Amos, how did the juke box work go?

Well, I went in with Mike and just walked over to the box and started smashing it up. He knew something was up because he didn't say a word. I left him the bat for good luck: I tossed it into the mirror behind the counter; broke a lot of bottles.

Good going, Amos. We're going to get along. I'll be in touch.

CHAPTER FOUR:

WHEN HAVING PROBLEMS, LOOK FOR A NEW START. (ANGER)

Foreword: Reincarnation is discussed and examined, as well as the importance of a good teacher when pursuing Yoga.

MIKE

Hey Vittorio, I got a big shipment from the market today. We must be rolling in the money now. Here's what we talked about:

VITTORIO

Just keep the raw materials moving to the pill makers.

ANDY

The Gita points out that **these teachings are rare in the world. Relatively few hear them and even fewer act upon them.** I think we are acting on them by discussing them between us. It's like we are witnessing each other's ideas and helping each other to understand.

AMOS

I think we are becoming aware of our strong, usually unconscious, motivations. Perhaps being shell shocked is a benefit that way; it works for me. There is no doubt in my mind about reacting to loud noises; the reactions are automatic and very strong, related to a survival instinct. Feeling like going to the bathroom is not something we make up on purpose either.

MIKE

I doubt if any of us have studied these teachings before. The nuns didn't teach anything like it. It's like going to a school that teaches about what's really going on in life, and we find out it's not what we think.

REINCARNATION

ANDY

Another idea is that we **constantly change and take up new lives even in this life.** We start when we move from being babies to being children to being an adolescent to being an adult to being a worker, to being married, to being a parent, to being old to being dead. Somehow we always consider ourselves to be the same "person;" we have become experts at fooling ourselves about reality. Another way the Gita looks at it is that **consciousness created four divisions of society:** the wise, the soldier, the merchant, and the laborer. In today's world this would be positions like (teachers and philosophers), (policemen, firemen and soldiers), (those working in stores or businesses), and (those working on construction or loading trucks or doing other labor). Sometimes we may move from one of these jobs to another, like you are doing now, Amos.

AMOS

Yea, when I was in the war, even in the worst of it I always felt that it was the same me. I knew that I existed. That seems to be the only thing I can say about myself for sure, and when I do I'm not sure that that idea referred to my body; it was just a sort of "knowingness." But, going into the army was stressful and coming out of the army is stressful. Perhaps when we stay in the same kind of work we avoid stress?

MIKE

When I wake up with a hangover, I still know that I exist. Does my horse know that it exists? Maybe it's just a feeling rather than idea. Horses don't have verbal ideas. We are finding out that our ideas don't seem to work very well either; otherwise I wouldn't get hangovers in the first place.

THE BODY/MIND:

ANDY

We are not the body or mind-these are changing continually. When something is constantly changing there is nothing we can point to that continually exists. We don't give a name to a wave, unless we are a surfing. The new thing is not the same as the old thing. We know that, but ignore it when looking at the slowly changing things around us. Practically, in this reality, we do what we have to do, but we don't remember that it is only using conventions. This is normally not important, except when we are trying to be accurate about what we really are. What we are is often considered to be consciousness, the Godhead. But those that know say that we are the pure awareness that makes consciousness conscious. Reality starts with a granular cloud that is permeated with the light of pure awareness, and then something vibrates starting space and time. It takes a lot of training to really see that. The information has to come in many different forms until we finally **see** what it means, or accept what we know to be true; this knowledge, however, is experiential, so we are having difficulty talking about it.

AMOS

Even war does not exist as a thing. It keeps changing. The whole thing is just a concept that allows the fighting to continue. The fighting, itself, constantly changes, obviously. But in that reality we are required to pay attention; it is our job; just like when crossing the street and traffic is coming. Well shell shock teaches you quickly that you're not in any kind of control of your body or mind. They are out of control and depend only on the circumstances. I react to all kinds of things that appear to be a threat, from loud noises to people running or dogs barking, and I don't know how to stop the reactions.

MIKE

I've had this horse for a long time. I saw it when it was young and I had to train it. I taught it how to respond to signals. All its reactions had to be learned. When it learned them, it changed and became a "new" horse, worth more. What's more, I had to learn how to teach the young horse. The whole system goes back to when horses were first domesticated. We learn and change the same way. Then, when we go to get a job, we are worth more. I can see how I was changing as I grew up. Now that I am a man, it's more difficult. I know what the words mean, but it's hard to understand. It's easier to see my mind changing: first I'm hungry then I want a beer. I have thoughts going on all the time; they even make it difficult to fall asleep unless I have a couple of beers, or a little muscatel.

GOD UNION:

ANDY

What we are learning here is to **realize that we are one with God. Even the Catholic saints such as Theresa of Avila claimed that the Godhead is within us.** This God is not an old man in a white flowing coat. It is pure consciousness, the knower in each of us.

In grammar school this was not taught. I suppose they felt that we were too young for this kind of teaching. If the Godhead is within us, how could we or our soul go to hell? There's a mystery there. The Gita also says **whenever spirituality decays and materialism is rampant, then, these teachings come back.** They are brought back because of suffering, which automatically raises consciousness in an effort to solve our problems.

AMOS

If they say that the Godhead is within us, and is only consciousness, we might as well say that all this is God. I can accept that, but I don't understand it conceptually. If this is all God, and we are obviously part of it then we must be angels. It is beyond the mind, but I hope it is not beyond what we can experience. It seems like others have experienced it if they have written books about it.

MIKE

If it only depends on experience to know it, let's try for it. I'm willing to do whatever is necessary, watching my motivations, selfless service, meditation, study, or practicing compassion.

WORSHIP:

ANDY

If we take some other path, the Gita says **for success in the world, worship the gods of the world.** I think that refers to the way we treat our homes, cars, and even our work and many other things. All these things require a lot of our attention, time, money and other sacrifices. This gives us practice in worship which we will eventually use for a higher cause.

AMOS

Don't forget the God of war. Our country worships war. We sacrifice our children, money, raw materials, time and political life. That tops any of our individual gods. That's the god of our world; sports come in a close second.

MIKE

Well, I'm involved with the mafia Don, Vittorio Calabrese. He's at least the high angel of a lot of people by that definition. Even the police do what he asks. He controls a lot of money, what plays on the jukeboxes, what area gets drugs, and a lot of people's lives. He's pretty high up there as we measure our gods. And, you could say that the mafia worships family, money, possessions and other things that bring what we call success.

THE GODHEAD:

ANDY

The Gita refers to our consciousness as the Godhead within. It can be known through contemplation: deep concentrated continuous thought. We are all conscious, so we have direct access to the object of contemplation. We usually think of it as being conscious of something, like a car or a friend, for instance. The thing we are conscious of constantly changes, but consciousness itself is like the screen in a movie theatre: it shows whatever is playing, but is not affected; it remains pure. It can only "know" itself through inference.

AMOS

If consciousness is the Godhead within, we are already experiencing it, or, perhaps more accurately, it is the experiencer, who/what we already are. Consciousness is what knows all our perceptions and thoughts. That's the point of all this discussion. It's easy to say, but not so easy to know for sure. I think we first have to eliminate thinking about other things as our self, like the body, thoughts and feelings. A better description is that the body is our "piece" in the drama of life.

MIKE

I don't see how the experiencer can experience itself. It's like the eye seeing itself. Wait a minute; it's not the eye that sees, but it only receives light and turns it into electrical impulses that are sent to the brain. But, knowing that all these perceptions and thoughts are actually experienced tells us that they are not us; they are all part of nature, including bodies and minds. We are not what anything that is experienced; at least I don't think so. Perception is moved to the mind and becomes conscious. It's confusing because the experienced is only known as it exists in consciousness; it appears to be made of consciousness. What else can you conclude?

PURIFICATION:

ANDY

It's recommended that we purify the self in the fire of the (upper) Self. This means to me that we find out what we strongly want or don't want and then resist these impulses with all our force and intention. This covers all parts of our lives including food, work, friends, sex, money, etc. We are the laboratory where purification takes place. We start with giving up the obviously bad habits: drugs, alcohol, coffee, smoking, and sugar. We may stop sex for awhile. It's all individual and no one is checking up on you but the (upper) Self.

AMOS

Since I came home I've been self medicating using alcohol and cigarettes. I don't know if I can give them up. But I'm going to try starting with one and see how it goes. Maybe I'll try sleeping less, at first.

MIKE

I've wanted to go on a diet anyway; that's where I'll start. I might even try fasting for a few days. I don't know if I can give up sex, or even muscatel or beer.

CONTROL OF ACTIONS:

ANDY

Another objective from the Gita is to **control actions by the (upper) Self. This includes both physical actions and thoughts.** That means, to me, that I have to watch my motivations and thoughts and avoid simply reacting to what goes on around me. From time to time I will do something out of the ordinary like getting up in the middle of the night and taking a walk or going outside and looking at the stars. Maybe I'll take a trip out to Wheaton and join the Theosophical Society.

Also, the Gita says **h**e who can see inaction in action, and action in inaction, is the wisest among men. I think that this means that to know that something is moving, there has to be something else that is not moving to compare it with. Also, what is going on is really the play of nature, it is not real. Things that seem to be standing still are really moving, like a slow wave; all things start as part of the earth.

AMOS

I'm pretty anxious since being discharged. I'll quit smoking and see how I react. It will take an (upper) Self even to think about quitting, let alone to actually do it. Hey, if I quit smoking that is an action that happens by not doing anything: (inaction).

MIKE

I think it takes an (upper) Self even to listen to this wisdom. It makes me kind of shaky just to hear about some of this stuff. Is listening or paying attention an action?

HUMAN DIFFERENCES:

ANDY

This instruction seems extreme: **give up the idea that you and I are basically different; our bodies are all made from this earth. Most importantly, our consciousnesses are identical.** It means that the real upper (Self) is the same in all of us. We are all the same, in our hearts. It seems that it is much easier to say it than to know it. It is like a hint or a pointer to find the consciousness within that is impersonal, much like a movie screen, and then act from this level.

AMOS

I can see that if we are watching our motivations and resisting them, in some cases that the resistance can only come from a self that is not part of the habitual self. It is impersonal, by definition. It might even be considered a little schizophrenic: the Self is watching the self or watching (witnessing) thoughts, actions and even perceptions.

MIKE

How about the duality of me and my horse? I can see that it is not really mine, because that's only a legal definition. I get it: the "I" is only a made up conceptual/legal notion, and so is "my." There is an ever changing body/mind but saying that it has some sort of absolute existence don't work. It would have to live forever and to have always been.

NATURE AND GOD:

ANDY

Another hard to understand concept: **all this is only nature acting on nature, but this altogether, when consciousness is included is God.** I guess that if all this is only known in consciousness, exists in consciousness, and then we don't know anything about any of it. We might as well call it all God. I have trouble giving up my ideas of God as being an old man with a white beard.

AMOS

When I remember back to the bombs going off and the shooting, it might as well be God. There was so much going on at once it seemed out of control. Even our religions approve of the fighting. Maybe that's why? I guess none of it means anything.

MIKE

You think you have trouble; I have trouble seeing my horse as God. But, if all this is God, the horse is nothing special compared to everything else which is also God. God is even in the addict's needle.

ANDY

To really know this stuff the instruction is to **find someone who knows and follow the path of yoga.** I guess the Theosophical Society is in my future.

AMOS

I'll wait until you let us know how it works. Meanwhile I'll follow my intuition.

MIKE

I think I'll just follow the path of my horse. I learn something from my customers every day.

VITTORIO

I get **angry** about the idea of giving up what's mine, but I'm starting to see some of the other points being made.

You have to know what you're doing; things have to run right; if things fall apart; there's always someone to take your place; not in a good way. Hey, bring Amos with you tomorrow.

CHAPTER FIVE:

PAY ATTENTION TO YOUR ACTIONS.

Foreword: Action, reaction and renunciation (giving up caring about results) and their respective merits are clarified.

MIKE

Hey Vittorio, I got a big shipment from the market today and moved it to the pill people. Here's what we talked about:

ANDY

Another issue brought up in the Gita: **is it better to give up our normal routines or should we make a practice of selfless action?** It seems to me that we always have some kind of routine. Practicing selfless action seems possible, but we always seem to expect something from what we do. Most people have to work to earn a living. Can any work be done as selfless action?

AMOS

I haven't been back for long so I don't have much of a routine developed yet. It's like me going around the old neighborhood seeing my old friends and even family involved in drugs. I feel I should do something to stop it all, and I expect my actions to help. But it would make me feel like I had done something that was good. Being a do-gooder is not exactly selfless. I would probably have to kill a lot of the dealers and some of my own family as well. How could I decide what to do?

MIKE

Well, I don't have much of a choice. I make a living going around to the neighborhoods selling fruits and vegetables and drinking muscatel as I go. That part of my routine is fixed. I could give up the drinking part, I suppose. Selfless action is easier for me to do: I just give some extra stuff to the poorer people. Even then, they often look at it as charity, which rubs some of them the wrong way. They don't like me for it, but I do it anyway, and even make a special point of giving extra to those I don't care for.

WISDOM, ACTION AND KNOWLEDGE:

ANDY

Are action and knowledge the same? When I do something, I know it; when I study something, I remember and know it; when I experience some event I know what happened. I just got it; action and knowledge are both occurrences' in consciousness. Knowledge is not thinking. We can choose to act, but knowledge comes whether we choose or not. The Gita also says knowledge reached by wisdom is attained through right action as well. I think that this points to the value of experiential knowledge. When we live our lives by doing what needs to be done, we will discover our conditioning experientially. This is better than a conceptual understanding just like learning to ride a bike by practicing is better than trying to learn how to ride by having someone explain it.

AMOS

I see. They could either hurt or help you: the wrong action and you get in an accident; the wrong knowledge can also cause trouble in life.

MIKE

If I take a day off people are not able to buy the things they need; if I think they want strawberries and they really want sweet corn they still don't get what they need. So it's not just a concern for the thinker/actor it's a problem for the people they may have an effect on.

PURIFICATION:

ANDY

When purified we see the self in everything and know that we are not the actor. We can still make choices about our actions and thoughts, although we usually just follow the conditioning. Conditioning is usually just the automatic interpretation of the body sensations as "feelings:" like/dislike, act/don't act, avoid/grasp. The problem is that habits and conditioning motivations are usually not in language from necessity as the linguistic explanation for the right brain would be an overload that would preclude instantaneous decision making. I guess that means that if we are actually just part of nature, then all the rest of this universe is also just part of nature, going through its normal action/reaction routines: all action produces a reaction, and motion is continuous.

The Gita also says renunciation of action and the path of right action both lead to the highest; of the two, right action is the better. Since we are a conditioned part of nature, when we practice right action, our conditioning becomes visible; our minds will complain and resist. Without that practice **we are deluded because wisdom is submerged in ignorance like a cloud hides the sun.** Renouncing action means going into prolonged meditation. Not many of us are able to do this.

AMOS

If this is all part of nature going through what might be expected, then there are no good/bad, except for how we choose what goes in which category. I was thinking about the war as being negative only making corporations wealthy and now I can see that people were only doing what they were conditioned to do. Conditioning got us into it and conditioning allowed us to end it. Also, that was just my way of making something wrong by taking a simplistic guess at motivation in an extremely complex situation. Since right action is just doing the work in front of us without any second guessing; that eliminates confusion and stress in our lives. I can now see that all of life is extremely complicated. Sometimes we have more than one thing to do and we have to choose. Usually we go by some kind of justification based on how we "feel."

MIKE

If all that is true then how drugs affects our friends and neighborhood is only something we define as negative; they start by wanting to release stress. Our friends living and dying are only events in consciousness. I can see it as being true, but I can't bring myself to accept it. This study group is starting to change my mind. Just like it says, our minds are always changing. Also, we never know the long term effects of any situation. It's best to just do our jobs and hope that we can be awake enough so that we notice our conditioning when our minds resist or when conflict comes up in life.

ANDY

The path of service leads to self-purification. When I was an altar boy, I felt good about it even though I had trouble getting up so early. When I look back I understand that the "trouble" getting up early was just some of my conditioning getting exposed. Without this teaching I wouldn't know it. For awhile I even thought of becoming a priest. The idea wore off when a mafia guy passing the collection plate got upset when I didn't have any money. He made me stand in the back of the church. That's when I changed my mind. Now I know that that's just an example of how the mind is always changing.

AMOS

For me, being in the war was about service. I can even feel that there was some kind of self purification. I'm sure not the same person I was when I went in. It changed everything I cared about. I probably would have been a drunk or a druggie if I didn't join the army. Now there's no chance of that happening. But, now what am I going to be or do with my life?

MIKE

Selling fruit and veggies in poor neighborhoods is my service. I make enough to support myself, and I'm performing a needed service. And Vittorio and I are close.

GUNA NATURE:

ANDY

Acting, action, and cause and effect are all part of nature, the gunas; choice is an action. We think that we are doing things and that we are in control of our lives, but this says that we are not. We couldn't drive down this street in this wagon if the street wasn't built, if the wagon wasn't built, if we didn't have a horse to pull the wagon, and a lot of other things that had to happen. The whole history of the earth and its people has made actions possible. And, we think that we are the cause of things happening. Cause and effect are lost in the history of nature that has resulted in the present. There is no such thing as and "I" either. There are only ever-changing body/minds.

AMOS

Even the war had its roots going back into antiquity. The Catholic Church, for example, used its power politically and in other ways to make life difficult for the Jews for a thousand years leading up to Hitler's Germany. Before then they Waged wars against Muslim countries as a "sport" at least a half dozen times. All that has created a history of war that has motivated us to this day. It is something for which we (as a nation) are well trained (conditioned) through our continuous worship.

MIKE

I think that even Hitler was operating from his own conditioning. He was conditioned by the world around him, including the religious world of Germany. My horse is conditioned, much like Hitler, to turn when I pull on the reins. Who/what is pulling on our reins? It seems like the situations that we run into every day trigger things that we like or dislike and then we take action, only there is no absolute "we" that can be counted on.

IGNORANCE:

ANDY

Good, evil and reincarnation come from ignorance. Since the present day world has been caused by its history, good, evil and everything else must also be a product of, we might as well say, ignorance. This implies that if we learn something that removes ignorance that we free ourselves from our concepts of good, evil and reincarnation even though there is no absolute good or evil and there is no "I" to reincarnate, but reincarnation goes on all the time. And the Self that may or may not reincarnate is not a self as we usually understand the meaning of "I." If we learn a little of this teaching our conditioning will change and our life will be different. yu

AMOS

I remember being in the war. How would what I know free me from that evil? I can see that it is all just what's happening out of conditioning, but how would that help me? If I wasn't conditioned, perhaps I could have avoided the draft, but that was my duty. I might have been a better fighter and not have been afraid. Perhaps my fear would have been perfect fear? I suddenly see. Even the war is not absolutely evil. It just fits my idea of evil. I didn't like it, wanted to be out of it.

MIKE

I can see confusion about good and evil. We each make up our minds about what is good and what is evil. There are a lot of good men in the mafia, for example. When they violate some law, we could say that is illegal, but not necessarily evil. Some of our laws could probably be seen as evil, giving advantage to politically connected business or individuals or biased against the poor. Illegality is a concept that only lawyers understand, and even they don't agree on the legal strategies or the details of any specific case.

STOPPING THE MIND:

ANDY

A starting point is finding a way to stop the mind. We all have a continuous stream of thoughts that, at the least, distract us from what is going on in our lives. We are constantly interpreting what is going on as good, bad, like, dislike, neutral, etc. If we can't stop the mind's rambling, for at least a little while, we are doomed to be operated by our conditioning, whatever it is or however it changes. When the mind stops it provides a context for seeing what goes on with constant thinking: its automaticity.

AMOS

I think that drinking, at least, slows down the mind. But I don't think that counts. Sometimes, when I'm swimming underwater for a long distance, holding my breath, my mind is quiet, and I hear sounds from far away. It's eerie.

MIKE

I can see that conditioning is driving us. It's so strong that we would need a lot of help to stop the thinking process. How could we change how we feel about things?

VITTORIO

It's good to watch what you eat; I'm giving up pasta for lent; I always do something in lent; the mafia has always followed the church's teachings. You could say that I've been religious.

Hey Amos, I've got some more work for you. There's a bookie that works for me near the LaSalle Street Station. He's going to have a package for me. I want you to pick it up and bring it tomorrow.

OK, Vittorio, I'll take care of it. See you then.

CHAPTER SIX:

CONTROL OF THE MIND IS REQUIRED TO ADVANCE EVOLUTION.

Foreword: Ashtanga yoga is discussed along with techniques for controlling the mind.

MIKE

Hey Vittorio, here's what we talked about today:

EXPECTATIONS:

ANDY

How do I work without expectations? Our actions always seem to involve expectations, otherwise we wouldn't do anything. There is always what we consider routine: eating, sleeping breathing, etc. But, deciding what to eat, what time to go to sleep, all depend on some kind of expectation or driving force or needs we react to and therefore we expect some result from our actions. To work without expectations is very difficult. But the Gita says that renunciation is in fact what is called Right Action. No one can become spiritual who has not renounced all desire. This is done most simply by a combination of service and meditation.

AMOS

It seems to me that you would have to get to a point in life where you just didn't care anymore. Old people, sick people, and others may feel like this. When you are really committed to a cause and give it everything, like being in the war, and get some finality, you get to feel like this. It can only be described as "I don't give a shit." At that point you have renounced everything, but still do your duty because you have a life to live.

MIKE

I know that when you expect to get something from what you are doing in life, it's a recipe for disappointment. I've failed at almost everything I've done; here I am barely making a living selling fruits and vegetables. If I didn't have a mafia connection I'd be done for.

TWO PATHS:

ANDY

I think that we have to start somewhere. **One path is selfless service and another is stillness and peace.** I think we all can understand selfless service. We can make subtle mistakes, like helping someone out because we want to feel good about ourselves. This is a way that our expectations get a grip on us. It needs practice. Selfless service with an old organization is probably the surest way to expose your conditioning. Just go all out and watch what feelings come up.

AMOS

That was a benefit of spending all that time in the army. Most of us volunteered to serve our country. We did feel good about it though. Training takes a lot of that feeling away; fighting takes it all away. The fighting wears you out until you "don't give a shit" anymore. Maybe that's the point.

MIKE

I think you have to practice selfless service until your expectations wear out. It's like donating to the poor. At first you might have some expectations, but eventually they wear out. Then, you seem to become focused, and somehow more efficient, and even effective.

ATTACHMENTS AND DESIRES:

ANDY

Letting go of attachments and desires can bring one to the realization of God Union. I can see that if we make a list of the things that we like and gradually give them up, a big change will happen in our life. Our routines would change, for starters. Then we would pick out new things to occupy our time. We would no longer be able to hide behind a planned, comfortable life style. Things would get kind of shaky. It's hard to see how it results in God Union. **To him who has conquered his lower nature by paying close attention consciousness is a friend, but to him who has not done so, it is an enemy.** Discovering our conditioning through experience is a critical part of purifying our minds.

AMOS

I can vouch for the shaky part. Getting out of the army leaves you in just that kind of position. You don't know what to do or what you want to do. You have to make it up, create some interests; you're already burned out: talk about not having expectations; that describes the situation perfectly. Perhaps the part about creating your life is close to the God the Creator idea.

MIKE

When you spend your days riding behind a horse, things get kind of quiet in your mind. There are still noises from people and traffic, but they don't occupy you much. It's like riding through a daydream. I've always done a lot of daydreaming in my life. Maybe daydreaming has something to do with seeing God. Things don't seem quite real, kind of heaven like, especially when combined with a little muscatel. Is drinking muscatel creating conditioning? I just got it: liking anything is desire; it creates conditioning and attachment. I'm already attached; muscatel is always in my pocket. I have to quit. It's obvious; the desire for alcohol and the way it alters my feelings clouds my consciousness.

FINDING REALITY:

ANDY

Stay focused in the present to find reality. If we stay focused in the present, then we don't pay as much attention to expectations of the future. We pay attention to what is going on: perceptions. **This is all one big perception (of everything we know) with a "voice-over trying to explain, justify, classify and describe what's happening, what's out there.** With all this that the mind does, it keeps secret the reasons for why it operates like it does. There is some kind of non-verbal structure behind it: conditioning, habits, desire, techniques for recognition, structures of memory and recall, and probably more.

AMOS

That was important during the war. There's nothing like the sound of bombs going off to keep you focused and alert and paying attention. It made awareness vivid. The vividness was all one thing moving and shaking.

MIKE

Daydreaming also gets all your attention. It is very pleasant, for me, and thinking doesn't interfere. It is unified as one perception. I feel as though I am in the perception and watching it at the same time.

THE SELF:

ANDY

Our task in this life is to find the Self. We have made up our mind that we are the body/mind; we don't know how to go beyond this habitual point of view. As a first estimate, **we are the consciousness** that is the aware part of a human being. It is what "knows" perceptions and thoughts. It's like the screen in a theatre. The movie doesn't change the screen; perceptions don't change consciousness. A more accurate description, using language to describe something that can only be known through experience, is that **we are the light of pure awareness; it is what informs consciousness**. The Gita also says that **the wise man is superior to the ascetic, the scholar and the man of action.**

AMOS

During the war, I had to watch out for my body, or I would soon be dead or hurt in some way. It's difficult not to pay attention to your survival. But in the immediacy of danger that concern sometimes goes away and you are just there with the show. That's when heroes are born; they don't care anymore. I think that heroes are also wise men for the time.

MIKE

I suppose that when I daydream or even when I dream when asleep, that is all like motion in consciousness. It is pleasant because I'm just watching without expecting anything; I'm just enjoying the show while I am also in the show. I just realized life is always just like that except we are not always enjoying it; it seems like we always have to be on the lookout for danger; we expect trouble. Giving up this expectation means we are giving up part of our conditioning. That will cut a hole right through conditioning an leave us space for right action.

BEING PRESENT:

ANDY

To train the mind to be present, find the right place, free of distractions; sit up straight, pay attention to the silent gaps between thoughts gradually expanding them. This is an instruction in how to meditate. I think it would be helpful to find a group that practices regularly with a teacher and learn with them. I heard that it is sometimes helpful to count the out breaths which gradually trains the mind to display gaps between breaths.

AMOS

I just thought that in our normal schooling we are never told that the mind needs training. We are told to learn things, but the focus is never on the mind itself. And when we look at how it works, it is basically out of control, doing its own thing, throwing up thought after thought, even when all that is wanted is to go to sleep; the mind don't stop easily.

MIKE

When I daydream, there are no thoughts. I'm just absorbed in what is going on. I mean there are no verbal thoughts. I see what's going on and am absorbed in the pleasant sensations that go with it. Being absorbed in sensation is much different than being the thinker.

THE GAP BETWEEN THOUGHTS:

ANDY

The Self reveals itself to awareness in the still gaps between thoughts. I think when the mind is still, the consciousness is still, so it is kind of like a mirror, reflecting the awareness back to itself. It is not covered by thoughts and is easier to discern. There's some kind of experience that is being pointed to here and words don't reach it. It takes practice to learn to control thoughts.

AMOS

I'm having trouble understanding this. I know what this is getting at, but it drifts in and out of my mind. If we keep our focus on the subject, maybe I'll get it.

MIKE

I think I see. When I am only feeling, it is the Self that feels, because it is happening right now. The mind doesn't remember the body's feelings the same way it may remember situations or thoughts, but the Self is only present to the "now" of direct experience. Normally we are distracted from the "now" by the steady stream of thinking that we habitually pay attention to. When we stop the thinking by placing our attention on some sensation, we are automatically focused in the "now." Verbal thoughts are always memory based.

TRAIN THE MIND:

ANDY

Train the mind, gradually, to rest in the silence of the self. This instruction points out that it takes training and it is a gradual process. I know that the yogis practice postures and breathing processes as part of their training. On the other hand, I've heard that sudden insight can happen that suddenly wakes us up. When the volatile and wavering mind wanders, restrain it (by the many meditative techniques) and bring it again to rest in silence. The Gita gives a test for wisdom: **He looks impartially on all – lover, friend or foe; indifferent or hostile; alien or relative; virtuous or sinful.** When we get to this point we are in pretty good shape.

AMOS

Well, it seems that all we can do is to keep talking about it to maintain our direction. I'm in for the long ride or whatever it takes.

MIKE

I guess I'll practice meditation or daydreaming whenever I get a chance. It's easy to be in the now when you feel the hard seat as the wagon bumps along. I wonder how meditation is affected by wine? It is a common practice in the bible, for example.

PRACTICE A TECHNIQUE:

ANDY

One problem is that meditation requires regular practice and development of an appropriate technique. I think if we stay alert to opportunities that we will find them. In the meanwhile we can try to develop a gap in our constant thinking process which is what meditation is all about, in the beginning.

AMOS

I notice that when I go out for a few beers that I expect drinking to make me "feel" better. It does, at first, and then it goes downhill, especially when I want to feel good more and more.

MIKE

I'm going to sit quietly every morning for five minutes before breakfast; I'll let you know how it works out.

VITTORIO

When I would do the rosary; I felt my oneness with God; I knew in my heart; that everything was OK; I still do the rosary sometimes. There are no problems in life. I never felt guilt about being in the Mafia or anything I did for the Mafia. And if I was angry, the rosary would calm me down. A lot of people talk about the Mafia and the harm they think it has done. That was just political talk. I was taught that being harmless is complex and perhaps impossible to know for sure except in the short term. You kill someone for some reason, perhaps you don't even know, and there is no way to know if it was for good or evil. We're not fortune tellers; we just do our assignments.

Hand me that package, Amos. Jesus Christ, he really wrapped it up. We're getting into a new business, this is cocaine. Here's $1000 for your help, Amos. Pass some on to your mother, and tell her hello for me. I keep track of all the neighborhood families.

CHAPTER SEVEN:

THE RELATIVE KEEPS MANIFESTING FROM PURE CONSCIOUSNESS.

Foreword: The absolute is discussed along with delusions of the relative.

MIKE

Hey Vittorio, everything's going good. Here's what we talked about:

DISCIPLINE:

ANDY

Use yoga for discipline and keep your attention on sensations and subtle body motions. Here's an instruction that's a little different. By yoga is meant hatha and pranayama exercises. It is a discipline, do it every morning and evening before meditation, like brushing your teeth. Do it automatically, without expectations. We need to insert some positive discipline into our lives. It lets the Self know we are paying attention.

AMOS

That is pretty easy; it's not abstract; you just do it. I'm going to use that approach. I'm also going to get some books from the library and start studying the subject. I'll make that part of my discipline.

MIKE

Hey, I'll add a stretching routine before sitting quietly every morning. Just doing it will change my attitude for the day. Can you get us something that describes the hatha exercises?

ANDY

Here's a Hatha page that came from a meditation course my mother attended. Massage and stretching is important to address the conditioned stresses that reside in our bodies. Each physical stress has a mental/emotional component that we can realize as we practice. Doing the breathing exercises is another route to become aware of how stress affects our breath.

THE DIVINE ILLUSION:

ANDY

Awareness sees what's true and not true, what's real and what isn't. This seems pretty mystical to me. I think it refers to, for example, when you see a rotten apple, you know its history: seed, tree, rain, sun, etc. You also know its future: into the earth again. But, I see that when we decide to practice yoga, intuition will lead us to whatever will teach us next. Or, if we make a promise, we will always know what we need to do to keep the promise. I just got it: what's true is what is, our perceptions, not what we think about them or infer from them. What we infer is a hypothesis that may be proven provisionally with other testing; the conclusions are never absolute. **This Divine Illusion of Phenomenon manifesting itself in the Qualities is difficult to grasp conceptually**; experiential knowing is required: yoga practices, meditation, selfless service, etc.

AMOS

It's like joining the army; some know it's a promise to perform and others flunk out. Going to college must be similar. We would know how to do justice to our selected studies. We just do what's necessary. That's what's meant by experiential knowledge; it's not what we learn conceptually, but how we learn. The "how" is the experiential part: do this and then do that.

MIKE

I see. I decided a long time ago that I would bring fruit and vegetables to neighborhoods where there wasn't much choice to help people eat healthy. One thing after another brought me to this horse and wagon and then the possibility of supporting me with a little side business with Vittorio came up. I just did what was right in front of me. It's been all experiential since then with a little selfless service added.

DIVISIONS OF NATURE:

ANDY

Earth, water, fire, air, ether (living space= awareness plus space), mind, intellect and personality are the eight divisions of nature. Beyond these is consciousness, the source of life. Most of us don't think of our minds as being a part of nature. The mind seems pretty active and what "it" thinks of as lifelike. Many automatic stimulus-response mechanisms seem lifelike: thermostats, power steering, power brakes, slot machines and computer games.

AMOS

Hey, all this exists in our consciousness so consciousness must be the source of everything. It's strange how I was able to state that fact. I just know that it is true.

MIKE

I think a healthy diet is one of the things that helps keep your consciousness clear and untroubled.

THE SPIRITUAL LIFE:

ANDY

The reasons for people coming to the spiritual life are: because of suffering, to understand life, to achieve life's purpose and because of accumulated wisdom. I think we are aware of suffering in our lives and in others. Now that we have started studying this yoga a lot of the other reasons seem to apply.

AMOS

I've seen suffering during and after the war in Europe. People lost everything, including their families. Now they have to make the effort to rebuild their cities. And there's plenty of poverty here, in the neighborhoods, that results in suffering. Look at all the skinny kids; they almost look like skeletons.

MIKE

I used to be one of those skinny kids. There was never enough to eat. I used to steal bottles of milk left by the milkman on the door steps. I don't remember thinking about suffering, though. To me suffering was a toothache or a sprained ankle. I think, now, that by suffering we are talking about something we don't like, or part of life that we can't change, for example when a relative dies, or you get fired from a job, or you have to move to a smaller apartment because you can't afford the rent.

CONSCIOUSNESS:

ANDY

Everything is in consciousness, and it is in everything. When we say that we are conscious of something, it means that we have consciousness. Not having consciousness means that we are unconscious or dead. The Yoga Sutras say that sleep is just a pattern on consciousness, perceived by awareness. Everything we perceive is known because of consciousness; these perceptions are all found in consciousness and nowhere else. And, **consciousness is the Life Force in all beings,** so we better pay attention to it; do what's necessary to increase consciousness.

AMOS

If all this is in consciousness, then it all must be made of consciousness. It's not like a boat floating on water or a submarine moving underwater. Hey, it's not our consciousness; it's more like we belong to consciousness or we are in consciousness. Without it we wouldn't exist. And, all consciousness is the same; it can have no bias like a movie screen can have no bias. There is only one consciousness; it is used by each of us to know our perceptions.

MIKE

Even horse shit is made of consciousness. This is getting me dizzy. I keep losing the point. Maybe it's the wine.

LOWER GODS:

ANDY

There are many lower gods. Worshipping them will unify consciousness. By lower gods, I think of the Catholic saints, perhaps even Jesus. But maybe there is worshiping that we normally don't think of; some people worship money, or food. The Gita also says **they who worship the Lower Powers attain them, but eventually find consciousness**.

AMOS

I think some countries worship war. We sacrifice our children's lives and our money and time and **attention** to war. It really focuses our attention. I guess when attention is focused, consciousness is focused; it has direction. That's where worship leads. But it also means that those who worship war get war.

MIKE

A lot of people really worship alcohol or drugs or other desires; they don't focus their attention, except for ways of getting more drugs. Maybe that's the idea. You tend to get more of what you pay attention to. When you own a business, even like this horse and wagon I have, it organizes your money and time. You become focused on the situation. If you don't own a business and only work in some factory your attention is not necessarily captured in the same way or with the same strength. I see that attention is pretty important in the practice of yoga.

NATURE:

ANDY

Nature has three qualities; the names are usually given as: 1) Rajas which can mean activity, energy, motivation, increase or action; 2) Satva which can mean intelligence, knowing, sensing, or interpretation; 3) Thomas which can mean inertia, stuckness, ignorance or resistance. We can think of these three qualities as 1) applying to people or things that cause change, 2) as people or things that accept change, and 3) as people or things that resist change. All three are always in everything. This deludes us all. We think that we are involved with life, but it is all nature acting and reacting, including our minds and bodies and everything and everyone around us, except for consciousness.

AMOS

In a way this is all just happening. There is no good or bad, there is only what we think about what we experience; it is all just moving and happening now, like a movie on a screen. It really gets us to pay attention, and then we think about it and we pay more attention to what we think than what we see.

MIKE

I guess we are all products of our history. We start learning as babies and then as we grow up. By the time we are adults we are done for; we are one big ball of habits. We like some things and don't like other things; we think we are right about our likes and dislikes in spite of what other people do or say or how much trouble it causes us. But, hey, if we start to worship something new, that changes our direction in life.

THE OPPOSITES:

ANDY

Beware of the opposites; attraction and aversion or desire and fear are the main cause of our being deluded with what this life is about; they keep our consciousness constantly stirred up. I can see that trying to get what we want and avoiding what we don't want can cause a lot of problems; we get habituated. Our minds are always busy planning and reacting and we think this is the best track for our lives. It leaves no room for creativity, for contributing something special to life. We are caught in a context that we don't see. The context is the present situation and all its history and innumerable causes, and what we think of them. The other, most important, context is not visible; it's consciousness.

AMOS

We all just keep running in the same direction we've been going because of our habitual responses. We need to lay some new track, if we want to cause real change to our lives. If I had studied some of this ten years ago, I may not have joined the army. Should a, would a, could a: if only we could change the past. I think this means doing some things on purpose, in the present, to accomplish stretch goals that we have set. I guess promises and commitments are important.

MIKE

I like some foods and don't like others. That is not what all this is about, unless my appetite causes me to lose health. I think we are talking about strong attractions and aversions. Some of us don't like authority figures. That can negatively affect your whole life. You probably will not like working for others. That's why I operate a horse and wagon. No one is looking over my shoulder.

VITTORIO

When there are no problems; you just do what's next; do what needs to be done; follow your family; don't be afraid to work; keep on going. What's next is always obvious. I get angry when I don't know what to do.

Hey, tell Amos to deliver this cocaine for me to the bartender at tavern on Laflin Street across from Cruz's pool room. I got to get him involved in the work sooner or later. I need guys that I can trust.

CHAPTER EIGHT:

THOUGHTS ARE IMPORTANT WHEN CHANGES ARE HAPPENING. VERY FEW OF US HAVE ANY CONTROL OF OUR THOUGHTS. A KEY ISSUE IS THE AUTOMATIC NON-VERBAL MIND MAPS THAT WE ALL HAVE AND DON'T KNOW IT, INCLUDING:

- Names bring up forms.
- Names bring up other names.
- Forms bring up style.
- Clothes bring up meaning.
- Appearances bring up possibilities, e.g. sex, work, etc.
- Sensation brings up meaning: e.g. like, dislike.
- Stimulus brings up response; avoiding a response is also a response.
- Conversations bring up overlapping mind maps from the participants.

- Walking brings up directions.
- Driving brings up directions.
- Driving brings up options for operations.
- Cleaning house brings up possibilities for efficiencies.
- Efficiency brings up many possibilities in life where maps are required.
- Preferences exist in maps.
- Swimming needs a map.
- Exercising needs a map.
- Linguistic accents and inflections imply a map.
- Vocabulary implies a map.
- Conditioning resides in maps.
- Habituation resides in maps.
- The "opposites" require maps.
- Classifications reside in maps.
- Perceptions have maps of like/dislike/neutral/survival.

These maps are not accessible with language. They are accessed by non-verbal reaction and result from conditioning that starts with the desire to relate to the world (parents?) with some level of control: walking for instance.

Foreword: This is about the importance of the last thought before dying/being born again, even in this life (new job, spouse dies, move to new home); the differences between the spiritual and material worlds; good/bad.

MIKE

Hey Vittorio, I got a big shipment from the market today. I had to leave some of the stuff in the horse barn. Here's what we talked about:

GOD:

ANDY

What is God? Or, as the Gita puts it: What is that which men call the Supreme Spirit, what is man's Spiritual Nature, what is the soul, and what is the Law? What is Matter and what is Divinity? I think the closest we can come is to say that God is all this, the entire universe and everything in it, including the apparent nothingness of empty space. And, when we take that statement in the light of what we are studying, **consciousness which includes all of material existence with the space around things is what we call God.**

AMOS

There were soldiers in the foxholes praying with their Saint Christopher medals and other tokens of Christianity. It's like some have said: there are no unbelievers in foxholes. I doubt that any God is worth praying to if you look at the history of war and calamities and the suffering of mankind. Perhaps it would be more accurate to say that God does not act to eliminate our fears, or to make our lives easy.

MIKE

I vote for consciousness being God. When you see that all this exists only in consciousness, as perceptions, it's pretty convincing. I wonder why this is not common knowledge? But, even now it keeps drifting in and out of my understanding.

ACTION:

ANDY

What is action? Action is just the way that consciousness expresses itself through nature, the gunas. **Consciousness has a tendency to express itself.** So we just keep rolling along with our lives, doing whatever is called for by our circumstances. Even thoughts are a form of action. What we do and what we don't do are both actions.

AMOS

That means that even prayers are just a way of consciousness expressing itself. And so is war. It's all just action that we label as good/bad/neutral.

MIKE

It's easy to see that it is just nature expressing itself when I watch my horse pulling the wagon, or the stars moving through the sky. When I decide to do something myself, it is much harder to grasp. I guess my view of nature is trying to exclude myself by putting perceptions outside of myself, not considering that I am my body in other's perceptions and therefore in their consciousness. This notion about action being performed by nature steps on some personal views. I don't like it.

GOD'S ACTION:

ANDY

Everything comes from God and God lives in every creature, this includes good and evil people, even Hitler and Stalin, even bugs, even trees. This is a lot easier to look at if we say consciousness is in every creature, in every thing. We know that is true. The word "God" is loaded with biases that make it difficult to discuss.

AMOS

Speak to me about the God that let the wars happen. A lot of it was just slaughter of innocent civilians when the cities were bombed. Just think about the atomic bomb at Hiroshima: about 250,000 civilians, old men, women and children died in minutes. At least we can see that consciousness has no bias and will let war or anything else happen.

MIKE

It's easy to become bitter when thinking that God lets all these miseries happen. If he didn't this would be heaven on earth.

ANDY

God's action is creation. I guess all this motion could be called "creation." None of this creation is permanent. Look at all the homes being built in the new areas where there used to be corn fields. That's creation. Look at the new designs of planes and bombs; that's creation for sure. If I could save a little money I'd buy a new car. Then I'd create a trip to California in the winter.

AMOS

I used to be a pretty quiet guy before the war. Now I'm riddled with anxiety. I suppose that being anxious is also some kind of creation. And, we're learning something critical here and that's also creation; all ideas new to us represent creation. I guess that all motion is creation, like a wave in the ocean becoming larger or smaller and having its influence on the water around it.

MIKE

Well, all this food continues to grow and is transported to the market so I can sell it all over the West side. There's a lot of creativity involved to find cheaper ways of doing it and how to keep everything fresh. We keep getting new varieties; it's all creation.

REINCARNATION:

ANDY

After death consciousness is left with unsatisfied, incomplete, active conditioning that exists as a pattern on consciousness. This continues as consciousness and its patterns don't die and are reborn in a new body. This is another aspect of creation. Some call it reincarnation. I guess that this ensures that there is some kind of continuity in human beings and the human situation. A lot of people think that this ensures that we will get punished for our "sins." But if we are just acting out our conditioning, and the actions are just nature doing its thing, where is the justification for calling anything a sin; where is the justification for calling anything punishment? It seems like a system that keeps going, ad infinitum. There is nothing that we consider an "I" involved, but there may be a higher Self involved where punishment is not a consideration.

AMOS

If I had to call anything a sin it would be war. And wars have been going on since humanity started. We know that many, if not most of them were not justified. Does this notion mean that we are doomed to start more wars in our next lives, and the next next lives as well?

MIKE

If I sell fruits and vegetables in this life, will I do the same in the next life? How do we escape the bullshit we have to deal with here?

LIFE'S CHANGES:

ANDY

Before any big change, like dying, moving, or getting a new job, meditate for awhile. Meditation is a way of going beyond the conditioning, for at least a little time. Practicing every day helps us to recognize conditioning so we can, at least, resist its influence when it comes up. At least we see what our current strong thoughts are about. We always bring our old conditioning with us. Often, the first time someone meditates they notice that their mind is constantly throwing up thoughts. That was always the case, but they never noticed it.

AMOS

I still have conditioning that was created in the foxholes. When I hear a loud noise, I duck. If I see an authority figure that looks like an officer, I avoid him. I hope meditation gets me out of this reactive life.

MIKE

You made me think that I have always tried to stay away from barber shops. When I was a child I had my ear cut. I wonder if I could make up a list of what I avoid? I also avoid football games. There are a lot of things that I don't like. I don't sell broccoli even though my customers ask for it.

BIRTH OF THE COSMOS:

ANDY

The cosmos itself is born and dies and is constantly changing. I know that some scientists say that the earth is only 14 billion years old; all this started with a big bang. Even our bodies are changing every second, loosing tiny pieces and gaining other tiny pieces. Even at the level of the cosmos, creation never stops. Consciousness is orderly.

AMOS

Don't forget that countries are always changing, sometimes at the borders and sometimes in other ways, for example washing into the ocean. Europe will never be the same after the war. Many countries with dictators now have a democratic government.

MIKE

The South Water Market is changing also. The congress expressway is letting some of the supermarket chains bring in their fruits and vegetables directly, bypassing the Market. More people driving cars lets them get picky about where they get their produce. My business is still OK because I supply mainly to the poor.

ANDY

God is the true self of all creatures, therefore pay attention to life. I think that "God" mentioned here is pure consciousness; it allows us to be aware of our circumstances, it observes our perceptions as a pattern on consciousness. Worship must mean devoting our time, energy, money and attention to what makes us more conscious. For example, yoga postures, breathing exercises, eating healthy pure foods, are forms of worship for yoga. In other words, stay healthy. Quiet meditation is the best form of worship.

AMOS

If it's like most things, it involves work, or you could say devotion: we are giving it our time and attention. When we are caught up in some avoidance action, we could say we are more conscious when we know we're what we're doing and less conscious when we don't know.

MIKE

So if I purposely go to a barbershop, just to make my body sensations involved with avoiding barbers become conscious, I would be increasing my ability to stay conscious. It follows that if we can make a list of all the situations we habitually avoid and then purposely expose ourselves to them while watching our reactions; we would be making ourselves more conscious increasing the God-quality in us. Hey, this would work for things we want as well: leave our favorite candy lying around, but don't eat it. Observe the sensations of desire. Our desire for sex would work the same way.

VITTORIO

After a time; the Latin words to the rosary are always in your heart; you know what's happening; you do what's right. What's right is never a question. In the Mafia, your boss will always clear up any confusion you might have about what the right thing to do is. How did Amos make out with the delivery?

He did good. We went right by the place with the wagon. He was in and out in no time. I think he's made for this kind of work. He's no good in regular work.

Bring him to me tomorrow.

CHAPTER NINE:

CONSCIOUSNESS IS THE SOURCE OF EVOLUTION.

Foreword: Consciousness pervades, creates, preserves, and destroys the entire universe.

MIKE

Hey Vittorio, I moved all the stuff into the pipeline. Here's what we talked about:

EVOLUTION:

ANDY

Unmanifested consciousness pervades the entire cosmos. That means that all of space and everything in it is full of consciousness. This agrees with scientist's findings that energy and particles keep coming out of empty space. Consciousness keeps manifesting yet remains. There is even a logical sequence to the manifestation: space, time, gas, fire, temperature differences, liquid, and solids.

AMOS

Well, the sun keeps producing light. The Stars keep moving around the heavens. I keep getting older. We keep inventing things like the atomic bomb.

MIKE

We keep growing new fruits and vegetables. I keep fixing the wagon and feeding my horse. My horse keeps pissing and crapping. The usual keeps happening.

WAVES ON CONSCIOUSNESS:

ANDY

Everything exists like a wave on the surface of pure consciousness. There are two issues here. First everything we know of exists as a wave. Our bodies for example gradually grow larger and then dissolve back into the earth. Everything on this earth comes out of it and returns to it. Since we only know things that appear in our consciousness they must be made of that consciousness. There is nothing that is outside of consciousness. It's like the appearances in a mirror are in the mirror; they are not somewhere else.

AMOS

Some waves move very fast and some very slow. Mountains change slowly as do diamonds. Light waves are fast. We could say it as everything comes and goes and comes again. Armies move slowly.

MIKE

The seasons are waves that we never consider in that way. They slowly come and go and come again, like day and night.

ANDY

The immature do not see consciousness as the creator; their lives are full of disaster and pain. I guess this is saying that we had better pay attention to consciousness. Another way of putting it is to say we should worship consciousness. Find out what makes us go unconsciousness in life and what strong emotions (like/dislike/anger/fear) overpower us and appear to condition consciousness. When we worship something it means the mind pays attention to it; we spend time studying it; we cultivate it; and we sacrifice our time and energy to it. We should "worship" consciousness; make peace, not war.

AMOS

I noticed in the war that fear made me hide in the foxhole when the bombs were going off. That hiding felt a lot how I hid from my father when he was beating my mother and she was screaming.

MIKE

It's the same way with me and the barber. That's fear. We need to face these things to identify the body sensations and where they are located and what specifically triggers them.

EMPTINESS:

ANDY

The immature live a life that is empty and meaningless. The Buddhists say that everything is empty of inherent existence, but still has relative existence. This is another way of saying that nothing is forever, everything is always changing (wave-like). But, we bring meaning to our lives. By our actions we interpret events, actions and feelings without knowing we are doing it. All of us do this. It doesn't favor politicians, world leaders, the wealthy, the religious, the old or the young. I suppose there are some yogis that are aware enough that they are in a class of their own. I wish I knew some of them. Maybe there are some people that understand this knowledge at the Theosophical Society.

AMOS

At least we know about it even though we are still stuck in a stimulus-response mode of living. We need to discover all of our stimuli so we can resist or go along with or consciously make a choice about our actions when it is important. I just thought we can overcome our conditioning, but we will just have new and improved conditioning more in line with our commitments when we are doing something. Making conscious commitments is one way to bring meaning to lives.

MIKE

We are on automatic pilot; we usually move through our lives thinking we have the freedom to choose when we don't. We are no freer than my horse. Anything we think of as being caused by a particular choice is a false concept. I couldn't drive the wagon down this street if someone didn't build the street first. The wagon and horse and many other things had to be in place as well. Choices can only be made in the context of pre-existing memories, conditioning and surroundings.

CONTEMPLATE THE SELF:

ANDY

The wise follow the path of Jnana (the intense study of...one consciousness in all.) This tells us how to improve. Jnana refers to a higher form of wisdom. There are no books that we could study that would tell us about how we are motivated in life; we have to examine ourselves to find out and then overcome the problems caused in our lives by their existence. But at least there are books like the Gita that give us hints about how to proceed and how to meditate, and critically, the distinction between thoughts and experience. One advice about how to start to know what meditation is like is to count the out breaths: breathe slowly and count at the end of each out breath. When the counts get to four, start over. Notice how the "space" between counts feels. That's consciousness. The advice from the Gita about this says to **pay attention to what you do, what you eat, and what you give up, even temporarily. Practice these things to make yourself more consciousness.**

AMOS

I'm just grateful that we decided to study this stuff. Does that decision make us Janis? I'm going to have to get myself a copy of the Gita to study. I'm making a list of the stimuli in my life that I recognize. I found that I need a list because my mind doesn't want to remember this stuff. It's starting to dawn on me. If consciousness is just the screen that existence shows up on then the screen is impersonal. We all have identical screens, or we all have the same screen, but hey, a screen is a screen and I'm glad I have one; or does it have me?

MIKE

I notice that some of my customers affect me: male or female, young or old, dirty or clean. I don't like mustaches: they make me angry.

THE WITNESS:

ANDY

Awareness is the inner witness. All our thoughts and perceptions show up in consciousness. All things have to exist in a space of not-thing so they may be known.

AMOS

I think what we are getting at is that there is no such thing as and "I." This can be hard to accept. Getting to acceptance is a big step. First you have to learn to give up a lot of cherished concepts/positions about life and reactions to life.

MIKE

It's the idea of the ego being a false thing, manufactured, and faulty in its working. It supposedly manages all our drives and motivations and false choices, etc. When I look at my horse there is no doubt in my mind that she operates with a stimulus-response routine. When I look at myself there is a lot of doubt. I trust what we are learning so I will work at it. Making a list of my strong emotions, including what upsets me, is a good starting point.

RITUALS:

ANDY

Those practicing religious rituals go to the heaven of their choice, and then they are reborn in this land of misery, sometimes referred to as "hell." When we first hear this statement we think of someone in church praying or going to mass, etc. Back when the Gita was written many rituals were practiced for better harvests, or to gain wealth or health, or for many heirs. In today's world if we are interested in wealth we get a job at the stock market or a bank or loan company where we work with and study how things work. This is the kind of ritual and practice we do today. And we do go to the "heaven or hell" of our choice every day when we go to work. After a long time we realize that our success does not bring happiness or decrease suffering. Then, if there is enough time left in our lives we look around and perhaps try something else. The Gita says about this: **Because they have sought but to fulfill their own desires, they must depart and return again and again.** We will keep getting involved in the same kind of stuff in this life and in the next.

AMOS

In that sense the biggest and most important religious ritual that we practice is war. We worship war; we sacrifice our children, money and resources to it. And, we never seem to learn, other than how to make new and better weapons. When we are not busy worshipping war, we worship other forms of violence like boxing, football and crime.

MIKE

The differences between nationalities seem ritualistic. I deal with Italian, Irish, Polish, Jews, and blacks every day. They all have their own manners and they all suffer. Even the mafia has its own rituals and traditions: the use of force and intimidation, the disregard of law, the acquisition of wealth and power, and much else. But, they get sick and die like all of us.

WORSHIPING CONSCIOUSNESS:

ANDY

Offer to consciousness food, sleep, exercise, suffering, sacrifices, service, etc. This will free you from the results of karmic conditioning, both painful and pleasurable. When we start to make changes in these areas we run into a lot of resistance from the mind and body. When we notice this, and pay attention to, the different thoughts and body sensations and attitudes that come, up we begin to get proof that we are not in any kind of control of our lives. It takes a strong commitment to practice this way consistently. The news doesn't seem very good to our egos.

AMOS

It seems that just by us studying this subject every day we have already started. Just this morning I didn't want to get out of bed to meditate before going to the South Water Market to buy the day's produce. I think part of my resistance was that my mind didn't want to think about the Gita teachings anymore.

MIKE

I know what you mean. This is a regular routine for me because I've been doing it for years, but I notice a desire to avoid the discussion as well. For me, it's more like an attitude of avoidance, like when a drunk comes up to the wagon and I don't want to deal with him.

THE PURE HEART:

ANDY

Keep your heart free and pure; purify your consciousness. To me this means that I don't wish anyone ill. I want everyone to find happiness, even the drunks I see hanging around the taverns across the street from the projects and throwing up and pissing in the alley.

AMOS

It's obvious to me that not many, if any, practice this. Just look at the wars, where we are encouraged, even by our religions, to hate the Germans, Italians and Japanese. We live in an Italian neighborhood so we don't have the "hate Italian," but I bet some of our relatives in other states do. We put the Japanese-Americans in concentration camps, for God's sake.

MIKE

Part of this is eating the right foods. If you eat a lot of hot peppers, you will get aggressive. If you overeat, you will get sleepy. When working with the mind and body health is considered important. It is difficult to get to freedom if you don't know that you are trapped by your conditioning; that is the situation we all find ourselves in if we don't work on uncovering our motivations: likes, dislikes, fears and upsets.

CONDITIONING:

ANDY

Anyone can follow this teaching to free themselves from their conditioning. It does not depend on education, wealth, sex, race or other distinctions. It is available even to criminals.

AMOS

I think that very few will try because they don't know it's a problem. It's only when suffering reaches a critical level that we become aware that we need some kind of help. Usually we just think something external needs to change: more money, a new boy/girlfriend, a new car, even a new horse. People never look at themselves or their minds as being source of their problems in life. If we do, we just think "I made a mistake," as if that makes it alright.

MIKE

I don't want a new horse. I don't even need more money, but I'll take it if I can get it. A new car would be good. I'd like to think that I'll live a good life, even if I do work for Vittorio.

VITTORIO

Our bodies need exercise; our minds need exercise; watch the breath; eat and sleep with care; go to mass on Sunday; say the rosary and pay attention

All traditions have a path for success; the Mafia's is selfless service, though I never heard it explained that way.

Here's something for you, Mike.

Amos, I have a different kind of job for you. Tonight, after you put away the horses, I want you to go to that tavern on Laflin Street that you delivered the cocaine; the bartender will point out a guy to you. Take this bat and break his legs.

OK, Vittorio. I'll come back and see you tomorrow and let you know how it went.

Skip tomorrow, but see me at Mother Cabrini Church before the 9:00 mass. You're going to help us passing the collection basket during the mass.

CHAPTER TEN:

EXISTENCE IS ALWAYS GOOD: WE LIKE THE DRAMA; WE CHEER FOR THE WARS AND THE SPORTS AND PAY CLOSE ATTENTION TO THE GOSSIP; THAT ACTION DOESN'T ELIMINATE SUFFERING.

(Bargaining)

Foreword: Consciousness is the location of all existence and is found with the senses everywhere.

Becoming more conscious will remove the clouds covering consciousness. Aspects to consider experimenting with are:

- **Postures**
- **Massage**
- **Rolfing**
- **Food**
- **Drink**
- **Exercise**

- **Breathing**
- **Studies**
- **Work**
- **Sex**
- **Fears**
- **Experiential and conceptual direction**
- **Sleep**
- **Meditation practice**
- **Meditation retreats**
- **Drinking enough water**
- **Vegetarianism**
- **Fasting**
- **Learning with groups: Yoga, Buddhist, Theosophy …**

MIKE

Hey Vittorio, here's what we talked about:

THE SOURCE IS CONSCIOUSNESS:

ANDY

We all come from consciousness. Since consciousness is the source of everything, this is obviously true. We know that we exist only because we are conscious.

AMOS

I noticed that in the foxholes when the bombs were falling I was much more aware of being alive and afraid of dying.

MIKE

We are discussing consciousness more than I thought possible. The more we talk about it, the less I'm sure of what I know.

THREE QUALITIES:

ANDY

The universe is made up of three qualities: motion, resistance, and purity. This could be explained in human beings as change, resistance to change and acceptance of change. Everything animate and inanimate has all three in varying amounts. Some of us are hyperactive, some of us are lethargic, and some of us are as pure as children. Even a rock is slowly changing while it resists change at another level and of course it accepts change.

AMOS

In war the activity is hyper. There is motion all the time. But a lot of the soldiers are dull from shock. Purity is not obvious to me. I think that I am changing as a result of this study group.

MIKE

At the Market, the people selling have big differences that are visible. My customers have the same differences. A lot of the Italian women are angry and expect to be cheated. Some of the kids look like angels.

REALIZE GOD-UNION:

ANDY

We are already in God-Union; we just don't realize it. Since consciousness is the source of and in everything, and it is another notion or word for God; we can see why this is true.

AMOS

Sometimes I think I grasp what we are considering and sometimes I think we are playing with definitions. So we are already part of God. I can live with that.

MIKE

This means that my horse is one with God as well. She is just God pulling God through God.

ANDY

Consciousness is worthy of devotion: give intense interest to it, study it, contemplate it and meditate on it. Well this is what we have been doing. We are interested in it; we are studying it; and then we contemplate the ideas that come up.

AMOS

It's the most important thing I've done since the war. I'm grateful that we happened into the Gita. Thank you, Andy.

MIKE

It's given me a new outlook dealing with my customers. It's like training in how human beings act. It's difficult to see the end of its influence on us.

RELATIVE EXISTENCE:

ANDY

This existence is referred to as "relative." Knowledge depends on opposites and arbitrary language relative to forms and abstract concepts without relation to the world of senses. We only know up in relation to down or here versus there, or mine versus yours, or big versus little, or abstract concepts like "good" or "fast" or "love" etc.

AMOS

I used to think of war as evil. But that concept depends on the definition of good. We would have to define an arbitrary scale going from evil to the greatest good. And, we would not be able to get agreement on any portion of the scale. For example: swearing, taking god's name in vain, having impure thoughts, stealing, fighting, cheating, killing, war, deserting war, etc. All these words require a detailed definition. There would have to be many exceptions, and even then any agreement would not be universal; it would merely be an agreement between "authorities."

MIKE

Even spoiled fruit depends on our knowledge of what good fruit is. Some fruit gets sweeter when spoiled. When an apricot dries out it is still good.

VITTORIO

Our world is made of God; the sun is made of God; God is night and day; he is the cosmos. When I am in mass I see the splendor of God's light on earth. Do you think that the Hindu books are as holy as the bible? I think God will accept all Holy books, but the bible **must be** the best. I **hope**

god understands my point of view; God knows everything, even our thoughts; God knows what's in our hearts.

Hey Vittorio, I broke his arm, OK? I had to run out of there. He had some friends with him. I'm lucky that Mike was outside to back me up. I think it dawned on them that I wasn't just some guy off the street. When they saw Mike, they just turned around and went back inside.

Everyone knows that Mike works for me. Here's a little package for you: good work!

CHAPTER ELEVEN:

HUMAN EXISTENCE IS APPRECIATED.

Foreword: The universal form is discussed.

MIKE

Hey Vittorio, here's how the discussions went today:

COMPASSIONATE GOD:

ANDY

Does God have compassion? I think that compassion is a human quality that some have and some do not have. I don't think that we can ascribe human qualities to God. On the other hand, god can have any possible quality because all qualities come from consciousness. The Gita also says that **consciousness is a creator as well as a destroyer whose purpose is destruction. But consciousness itself is never destroyed.**

AMOS

If God was compassionate it would be limiting. God does not have limits. We don't constrain God to giving us heaven on earth. Even our religions have aspects of evil in them. The church was playing politics against the Jews for a thousand years causing them untold suffering. They also empowered and justified many crusades against the Muslims. The operative concept was kill them all and let God sort out the souls.

MIKE

I agree. Only people have compassion and it is rare. God opens up all possibilities for human beings and other sentient beings: evil, good, indifferent, ignorant, wise, and many more.

THE LIFE SOURCE:

ANDY

Consciousness is looking out from us all; it is the life source in us all; we all understand what it means to say "I am conscious." We all exist in the perceptions of others, and we all perceive others. This seems so simple I almost think it is some kind of trick. The problem it presents is that it is consciousness is impersonal; our conditioning is the personal part and it is also what makes us human; we are usually not conscious of conditioning; it is both verbal and non-verbal. It means that consciousness has faces, eyes and bodies everywhere;

AMOS

We know it because we are conscious. It is an integral part of us. It is looking out of each of us. Some of us are mean and some of us are generous. The same consciousness is in each.

MIKE

The same consciousness is looking out from my horse and from all my customers. In that way I am all of them, and they are me. I feel that when I really know this, compassion will be automatic. We may not have the same idea of what compassion is at that point. Is pointing out someone's conditioning compassionate?

GOD IS EVERYTHING:

ANDY

All the universe is one thing: God, or consciousness. This takes a lot of contemplation to understand or accept. We know that from dirt we come and to dirt we go when we die. To think of the universe to be one whole integrated being seems strange. I guess it's no stranger than the heart, brain, and other organs we each have and consider to be part of us even though they each act independently to do their jobs.

AMOS

In the same way, I was just a small part of the war. If the war is thought of as evil, then I was part of evil. I don't like to think about it that way. I'm beginning to see that evil is just a human concept, and is always open to understanding and interpretation.

MIKE

Well I don't mind being part of a team that includes my horse, my wagon, my customers, the market, the farms, and the garbage men. It's all part of the universe, God.

PRECEDING EXISTENCE:

ANDY

God is consciousness; consciousness depends on the light of awareness; consciousness and awareness both precede what we call existence. When we open our eyes existence appears. The name "God" is used by religions without definition except to say that God creates existence: "heaven and earth." That is exactly what we know about consciousness: it is the source of space, time, gas, fire, liquids, and solids.

AMOS

Whatever we call by the name "God" assumes the power of creation, which appears to us as "magical powers." When we open our eyes and are conscious of the fact of existence; when our eyes are closed we still know that "I AM." That is pretty magical as well; we are just used to it. There is no difference in perception between sounds we hear and thoughts we think. The perceiver is identical in both cases.

MIKE

Hey, fruit and vegetables are coming into creation all the time. We don't call that magic. If anything, it's a form of manifestation that we depend on.

OTHER GODS:

ANDY

Other gods are also a part of consciousness and they also have powers. I think the old Greeks and others had the right idea. They had gods for war, love, death, time, and many more. And they had special sacrifices to get the gods approval. Some religions might call them "angels" wanting to have God as being separate from creation, and letting the angels do the dirty work.

AMOS

I've had firsthand experience with the god of war, and he or it is to be feared. We sacrifice our children's lives to it; we sacrifice our wealth to it; we sacrifice our money, children, time and attention to it; we worship it.

MIKE

I guess I'm sacrificing my time, part of my life, my attention and other things to the god of sustenance. I'm spending my life helping people get the food they need.

ANDY

When we see reality we realize that God-Union is just a state of fact. That's why it is called "realization." I see what it means. We have been told this by the statements in the Gita, but that is not enough to convince us. Our talking about it brings us closer to "realization." If we keep going, take up the practices of yoga, and study, the mind will eventually give up its resistance and we will "see" or "accept" reality as it is.

AMOS

When we open our eyes we see reality. What else could it be? The fooler is that it's all consciousness, which we never gave any thought to even though it's what makes all this possible.

MIKE

If I had control of the mind I would tell it to give up its delusions. After trying to meditate a few times I know that the mind just does its own thing, throwing up all kinds of thoughts even though I want it to stop thinking; to end thoughts for the time I'm meditating.

I AM:

ANDY

A more modern way of coming to this realization is by examining the primary fact of existence: "I am." That's the one thing that we can't deny: we exist. When we start to look at it seriously we find that what we are saying is that we are conscious; but consciousness doesn't fit our concept of a personal "I."

AMOS

Existence becomes very primary when the bombs are going off nearby. We just have to be conscious of them. Consciousness is required for anything and everything.

MIKE

I understand it as a concept, but I can't say that I have realized it yet. The mind still won't give up. I may have to make a sacrifice to the God of existence: time to study, money to buy books, sacrifice sleep to wake up early enough to practice meditation, and probably more.

VITTORIO

God is everywhere; he is in us all; he looks out of our eyes; he tastes our food; God or at least an angel is in the Mafia; He is a member of the Mafia! We are all angels.

Hey, bring Amos with you each evening from now on. He's a "friend of the family" from now on.

CHAPTER TWELVE:

THERE ARE MANY PATHS TO SPEED UP INDIVIDUAL EVOLUTION. THEY ALL LEAD ONE TO DEVELOP A GOOD HEART; BEING HARMLESS IS COMPLICATED.

Foreword: The path of devotion and other spiritual disciplines are discussed.

MIKE

Hey Vittorio, how're things? Here's our discussion:

VITTORIO

Hey Mike, first I want to tell you about what I did for selfless service. I arranged for some of my best men to serve as collectors during mass at Mother Cabrini Church on Sunday. They complained a lot, but I was able to persuade them.

WORSHIP:

ANDY

We should perform worship or search for a way to know consciousness. By worship is meant we work at it. This implies study and practice. This study group's discussion is a form of worship because we are spending time with and we are interested in the subject.

AMOS

I don't remember anything that has caught my interest as much as our discussions except for the bombs falling around my foxhole. This subject has to do with the foundation of what it means to be human.

MIKE

I agree. I've been involved with selling produce all my life and I thought I was supporting many lives with healthy food. The study of the Gita is more important to me than food.

CONTEMPLATION:

ANDY

Contemplation is a good way to know consciousness. As we think about the subject in depth, study some of the writings, and discuss our ideas with each other we are moving towards contemplation.

AMOS

I think contemplating the idea "I am" is a great way to train the mind to realize the truth of existence.

MIKE

I'm sold on this group study of the Gita. It is a fast way to test and refine our ideas about consciousness.

SELFLESS SERVICE:

ANDY

Selfless service is another recognized way to realize the truth of existence: this is all consciousness; all this is that. When we make a commitment to serve our own likes and dislikes become more visible. It is an opportunity to know the details of our conditioning. These details cannot be found in any book. They can only be found in the laboratory of our psyches in the process of living.

AMOS

Well I found out more than I wanted to know when I served our country in the war. Even before the war, in basic training I was constantly running into things I didn't like: food, sleep hours, working too hard, confrontations with sergeants, the way I wore my clothes, the way I make my bed, the way I walk around. I think that experience made it easier for me to grasp the importance of our focus here on the foundation of existence: consciousness.

MIKE

I remember many experiences that I have had just selling my produce in the neighborhoods. I don't like many of the people that I serve. I don't like all the care that my horse requires. She bites me every chance she gets; she steps on my toes. Some days I don't want to get out of bed, or I want to go fishing at Miegs Field. All those situations have body sensations and thoughts connected to them. They seem to be repeated again and again when I am reminded of those days.

STILLING THE MIND:

ANDY

Yoga starts with the stilling of the mind. I think we all see that our minds are not in control. Thoughts just keep on coming; the mind keeps describing our situations as like/dislike/fearful/neutral; we remember these situations, non-verbally by "marking" them with appearances, common ideas, sensations, and much more. We then habituate them as something to get or something to avoid. How the mind operates is not easy to know until you get into watching it and its operations. The Buddhists call it mindfulness, where the (upper) Self watches the self (ego). Most of what we are studying is just pointers about what needs to be done or studied next. Understanding the words is just a first step.

AMOS

When I remember the war, I know how the mind works, especially when it wants to avoid a situation. I felt like an ostrich that wants to bury its head in the sand and hide even though that will not help avoid danger.

MIKE

It's difficult to stop the mind when you are out in the world. I think some seclusion is needed to meditate. But, last Sunday I sat in at a Buddhist meditation center on North Clark Street. Meditating with a group helps, but up there an ell train goes by ever twenty minutes and young people congregate on the street below drinking beer and making noise. I suppose that a controlled situation works to some extent because, eventually, we have to bring the mind under some kind of control. We can't go on thinking we are the mind and leaving the mind to make all our choices in life. That's a recipe for suffering. True choices manifest as actions. Even thinking is a choice that we made long ago and forgot about. If we make a choice as a commitment it is extremely powerful.

GIVING UP DESIRES:

ANDY

Surrender of attachments purifies the self in the fire of the Self.
Giving up what we desire is very difficult. If we do it slowly, one at a time, the mind will gradually be tamed. The first step is to make a list; that's a choice to get started. Let's all stop now, and make our lists.

I can see now that surrendering attachments is going to be experiential. It's much more comfortable to just think about it and generate ideas than it's doing it. It takes practice to get the actual experience and know what it means and implies. Remember, experience is basically non-verbal; it consists of sensations, perceptions and thoughts that try to explain or justify it.

The Gita also says that **knowledge is superior to action, meditation is superior to mere knowledge, and renunciation of the fruit of action is superior to meditation.**

AMOS

Well I guess I can wake up an hour early and do some hatha yoga and meditation; then go on a vegetarian diet for awhile. I don't have to worry about giving up sex, since I haven't had any since the war was over.

MIKE

I'm used to getting up early. I can also become a vegetarian easily. I don't know if I could give up sex. I meet a lot of lonely women selling produce. I'll try it for a one month period. I can also wake up twenty minutes earlier to do some asanas. I'll have to remember to watch my thoughts; maybe I should keep some kind of diary; start with a list of attachments and include my experiences as they come up one by one.

BE FRIENDLY:

ANDY

Give up ill will; be friendly and compassionate. This is difficult for me because I have a habit of making myself better than others by making them wrong; it's automatic. I'll keep working on it.

AMOS

I'm still angry about the war-all the destruction and loss of life. You can only think that the political leaders of all our countries are insane. Otherwise we would all be in a rage; maybe we are all suffering from the same kind of insanity brought on by the gods of war. The problem is that most people agree with it all, like we are cheering on a football game. I'll work on that anger because it is very visible to me.

MIKE

On my rounds I meet a lot of people that I don't like. Some think I'm cheating, some are stealing from the wagon, and some are teasing my horse. Kids are always dropping firecrackers and scaring her. I guess I could notice the thieves and grit my teeth instead of hollering at them. That's probably going to encourage them to steal more. I can take the losses of a few potatoes or some sweet corn.

THE IMMORTAL CONSCIOUSNESS:

ANDY

Contemplate the immortal unchanging life of consciousness.
When we think about consciousness, which is a pretty unusual action in itself, we don't often consider that it never dies, and never changes. We know that human beings die, but consciousness lives on; consciousness exists out of time. That makes it pretty important weather we believe in reincarnation or not.

AMOS

I guess we should make this a formal period in our lives. I'm going to try it by adding a five minute period of contemplating (who or what am I?) after my morning meditation practice.

MIKE

Well, since my horse knows the route without my prompting, I can spend a lot of time in contemplation. It might get real when we get older people buying produce. I can see that they may not have much time left in this life. Time is funny that way: we ignore how a limited life affects us.

VITTORIO

The saints all loved God; it's hard to know what love is; we think of attraction as love, but, it's not, it's willingness to serve; when we serve, we are serving God.

The Mafia members all love God; our tradition has always been religious even though some forget their way. I noticed that when you get closer to God, you don't care much about anything anymore: everything is good; nothing is bad.

Hey, Amos. I got a real job for you now. Go with those guys in front of the house in the car. They are going to stop on a bridge over the new expressway. You take the guy out of the trunk and throw him off the bridge. Don't get caught.

CHAPTER THIRTEEN:

EVOLUTION COMES FROM CONSCIOUSNESS. IT IS ALWAYS MANIFESTING. (DEPRESSION)

Foreword: The difference between the transient physical body and the immutable eternal soul; individual consciousness and universal consciousness are discussed.

MIKE

Hey Vittorio, here's what we talked about:

THE KNOWER:

ANDY

What is the field of the knower? If consciousness is the knower, then the field must be thoughts, sensations and perceptions. Of course, there are other items in the field like choices and values, non-verbal conditioning and probably many factors we don't know about.

AMOS

When I looked out at the destruction on the battlefield I was dismayed. But life is like that: we have 100,000,000.00 dying every year of mostly natural causes. Death is not that big a deal. Consciousness exists as all of this; it witnesses this death merely as the ongoing change as a part of each human being.

MIKE

We place a high value on human life because we are biased. Plant and animal life support us without justification other than we are able to exert our authority, at least for the short time we are alive. I'm not so sure consciousness supports us entirely in this way. In the long term who knows what may happen (our bodies will return to the earth; this much of the future we can be sure of)? We may have to all become vegetarians.

KNOWLEDGE OF THE SELF:

ANDY

The Gita asks: **Who is God and what is Nature; what is Matter and what is the Self; what is it that they call Wisdom and what is it that is worth knowing?**

We have concluded that consciousness is what we call "Go;" it's not up for a vote.

The Gita also refers to nature or matter as: **The five great fundamentals (earth, fire, air, water and ether), personality, intellect, the mysterious life force, the ten organs of perception and action, the mind and the five domains of sensation; desire, aversion, pleasure, pain, sympathy, vitality and the persistent clinging to life.** I notice that if the intellect is just part of nature, then when we contemplate something, what is accomplished is questionable.

But, the Gita also says that the **constant yearning for the knowledge of Self, and pondering over the lessons of the great Truth – this is Wisdom, all else ignorance.** I guess that there is something here that we don't understand, **and that differences of character and quality have their origin in Nature only. Nature is the Law which generates cause and effect; consciousness is the source of the enjoyment of all pleasure and pain.** It appears that nature exists in a domain separate from consciousness. **Wherever life is seen in things movable or immovable, it is the joint product of nature and consciousness** The Gita follows this by saying that **nature and consciousness have no beginning.**

The knower in all of us is the witness, pure awareness: all this life, including consciousness, is known by this witness. Because of the past three weeks we have spent studying and discussing this subject, this information seems obvious to me. I know it on the level of information, but not on the level of direct experience. I guess I need more meditation and study. The Gita also says **some realize the Supreme by meditating on the Self within, others by pure reason and others by right action or service.** A Sufi once said: **when I don't know who I am, I serve you; when I know who I am, I am you.**

AMOS

I agree. I understand the words, for now, but that's progress, important progress. Knowing the meaning of the words helps us to follow our intuition to develop appropriate experiences.

MIKE

Now that we have some knowledge, we will automatically make choices that lead us in the right direction, to serve ourselves and life.

THE KNOWER:

ANDY

The knower is in all of us is non personal awareness which makes the witness possible. There is no difference in any of us at this level. Also, our minds and bodies are part of nature, which makes them non-personal as well: they are traditionally referred to as the three gunas: Rajasic, Satvic, and Thomasic,, or as sometimes described: action, resistance, and purity or causing change, resisting change and accepting change. In some sense there is no personal nature. However, we do consist of pure consciousness that is "colored" with conditioning we have acquired through many lives and added to in this life. This is the only part of a human being that can be considered personal, although it is much like the programming of a computer, or like the plays that a football team tries to complete. **When one of the gunas dominates a good or evil body may result.** We should try to become more Satvic and balanced.

And the persona types come out to seven primary possibilities:

NUMBER	PRIMARY TYPE	SECONDARY TYPE
1	Satvic	Rajasic
2	Satvic	Tamasic
3	Rajasic	Satvic
4	Rajasic	Tamasic
5	Tamasic	Rajasic
6	Tamasic	Satvic
7	All Three Balanced	

ANOTHER ANALYSIS:

	SATTVA	RAJAS	TAMAS
QUALITY	Purity	Action	Resistance
TYPICAL ACTION	Study	Compulsion	Heedlessness
DOMINANT TRAIT	Wisdom	Desire	Sloth
WORLD OF REBIRTH	Pure	Physical Labor	Ignorant
FRUIT	Selfless Service	Suffering	Insensitivity
RESULT	Understanding	Greed	Confusion
LIFE DIRECTION	Upwards	No Direction	Downwards
CHANGE RELATION	Accepts	Causes	Resists

AMOS

Our conditioning is personal in the sense that it is what makes us all different. It is still a jail that we are bound to as long as we are not aware of it.

MIKE

In some sense we are the same as my horse. She is composed of the three gunas and conditioning as well. Maybe that's why we often call someone "a horse's ass."

MOTIVATIONS:

ANDY

Here is a good question: **Are all motivations part of nature?** Now that we know about conditioning, it is hard to see any other motivating factor. A choice to perform selfless service may be in this category if it reveals some aspect of our conditioning. The higher self is not conditioned.

AMOS

Going against the grain of our motivations should not be described as part of nature. Conditioning operates automatically out of necessity. Our actions are too complex to bring into total awareness. Even something as simple as walking to the kitchen cannot be explained in language. When we are authentic we make choices while being indifferent to motivational conditioning.

MIKE

I think you're right. My horse never fights her conditioning, unless she's sick or has a conflict with some outside influence. When she wants to piss, she does.

MISERY:

ANDY

Why is there so much misery in our lives? I think that when there are a lot of conditioned operators there is automatically a lot of conflict.

AMOS

Sometimes we learn something important from the conflict. I probably wouldn't be here with you guys if I didn't serve in the war.

MIKE

Yea, it's like breaking the rack when you're playing pool. The balls have their initial conditioning; then they hit the banks and each other so the conditioning of each ball keeps changing. It's rare for one ball to stay in place on the break without changing, but it does happen. I think pool is a good metaphor for life.

CHOICES:

ANDY

How do we make choices in life? A true choice is known by experience when it goes against our conditioning. After some experience with the action of choosing we get to know choosing by the experience of being present. **It is only the Law of Nature that brings action to fruition; the Self never acts.** Choosing takes place, for or against conditioning, but always depends on the existing history of the universe, or God.

AMOS

I think, after we practice choosing for awhile, perhaps through selfless service, or through watching our mind operate, we get some kind of experience and can know better.

MIKE

That's the difference between my horse and me. The horse always follows my direction, and is rarely in any conflicting situation, except, perhaps when she is heat. I get to make a choice whenever I am in conflict. Sometimes I am afraid to do what should be done. I can choose selfless service; for instance, even when I think I'll get mixed up in some strange aspect of religion. I don't do it because becoming a priest would change the rest of my life. Joining the Holy Rollers is also like that.

OPPORTUNITIES:

ANDY

Where do opportunities come from? I think that there are two types of opportunities: the opportunity to satisfy part of our conditioning and the opportunity to go against some part of our conditioning. But, either kind comes from nature, the gunas.

AMOS

So life is just one big feast of opportunities. Somehow I don't feel like the war was an opportunity. But it is too recent in my experience. I don't have any perspective on that time frame. This discussion group is a special opportunity. Where did it come from?

MIKE

First, someone had to write the Gita. He had to know this stuff. Then it had to get commented on and translated into English. Then Andy's mother had to leave it around for him to read: And then, and then, and then, without a foreseeable beginning or end. The whole universe was involved in forming this group at this time in this location.

ONE CONSCIOUSNESS:

ANDY

Is consciousness the same in all? An analogy can be made comparing consciousness with a movie screen. Any part of existence can appear in the screen of consciousness. Consciousness itself is pure. We all have pure consciousness and there is no difference between the consciousnesses in any of us. And, this pure consciousness is eternal, unchanging, out of time and accepting of all, which is a definition of absolute love.

AMOS

Does that make us all twins? Are we all alike in our hearts? Is our conditioning the only difference?

MIKE

Well, I can see that I'm different from my horse. I have types of intelligence that the horse doesn't have. Our senses are different from animals. Some senses are better and some are not as good. But since I've been studying the Gita, I've come to believe that consciousness is all one. Our conditioning makes our life a good analogy with a pool game as we said. The balls move around the table hitting cushions and each other. They are conscious but very conditioned so they go on their way until they run into something and then their conditioning changes and they go in a different direction. Then one of them falls off the table of life until the entire game is over when they are put back on the table again. What they are not aware of is the player with the pool stick that puts a directed energy and intelligence into the game. That's why life is so full of suffering. We move about as conditioned beings until we have a conflict. Some conflicts escalate and others don't.

ACTIONS AND DESIRES:

ANDY

Where do actions come from? I think that actions come from desires. As a baby we cry when we are hungry or wet. We learn to try to satisfy our desires as we grow up and develop a routine trying to avoid what we don't want and to get what we do want. Like it or not all actions are choices made by nature. There is no "I" that is acting.

AMOS

I think the strongest desire of all is the desire to survive. In the foxholes, hunger and comfort are not near as strong as the fear you feel when the bombs are falling.

MIKE

Even my horse gives out signals about what she wants. When she's in heat she makes all kind of noises when she's around other horses, and she becomes very difficult to control.

SIN:

ANDY

Does the Self sin? The (upper) Self cannot sin. It is only the witness. All action is performed by nature, the three gunas: motion, inertia and knowing; sin is a human concept without connection to the actual world.

AMOS

I always think of myself as acting. I try to get things I want and to avoid things I don't want. That must be the lower self, the constructed ego.

MIKE

I'm involved in sin from time to time. Growing up Catholic I had a lot of sins defined for me in grammar school: swearing, taking the lords name in vain, missing mass on Sunday, and many more. I no longer think of those actions as sinning. The whole idea of sin has become very abstract. If I was defining sins I would start with starting wars. Think of the river of death that resulted from World War Two.

AWARENESS:

ANDY

Is awareness the same as consciousness? I've read that awareness is like a light that penetrates all of existence. When awareness is in anything, and it is in everything, then consciousness is the result.

AMOS

So, even the bombs falling and the explosions that result all have consciousness since awareness shines through everything? I think I can answer my own question: I can see that they do.

MIKE

Is there consciousness in the beef sandwiches that I eat? Maybe that's why I feel different after eating a beef sandwich than after having an ice cream Sunday? I got it. Our food is also composed of the three gunas and we gain in the predominant quality of the food we eat. We still have consciousness, but our (lower) self is biased in one way or another. Meat is heavier (more inertia) than fruit (light); hot peppers inspire motion.

VITTORIO

All this is just appearances; our thoughts don't mean anything; our feelings don't mean anything; appearances are empty and meaningless; we bring meaning to our world for ourselves. I used to get **depressed** when I thought deeply about religion and philosophy. That's when a little heroin is tempting.

The mafia has its own rules; they are as strict as any religion. They are kept.

I threw the guy off the bridge, Vittorio. No problem. Just let me know what you need and I'll do it.

You're a good man, Amos. I'll have a little work for you once in a while, but you'll be on a regular salary from now on. You're in the family.

Chapter Fourteen: Because conflict is always happening, evolution is develops; war is the most obvious of the many types of conflicts.

Foreword: The three modes of nature: **purity**, **passion** and **inertia**, their causes, characteristics' and influence on a living entity are discussed.

MIKE

Hey Vittorio, this stuff is getting hard to understand. Here's what we talked about:

WISDOM AND KNOWLEDGE

ANDY

How is wisdom different from knowledge? We get a lot of knowledge from what we read. Some of it is trivial, like reading for entertainment. Even studying to learn a subject like mathematics or a foreign language does not develop wisdom. I'm just starting to realize that our discussing and contemplating the Gita is one way to develop wisdom.

AMOS

I would have been wise to avoid the army and war. But, I don't think that is the kind of wisdom we are talking about. The start of wisdom is learning that you are conditioned and what your conditioning actually consists of; books only point to this; make a list of your own: likes, dislikes, upsets fears, etc.

MIKE

Even to get to that point you must first hear about this stuff, and then you must act on your knowledge. Knowing about it is not the same as acting on the knowledge. After acting on it, knowledge of the experience changes your conditioning, your nature. Your beliefs and values shift, and that shift is the beginning of wisdom.

LIFE AND CREATION:

ANDY

Where does life come from? When we see life our position is seeing something that already exists. We know about reproduction. I remember reading that time and space come from consciousness; they are the first vibration or manifestation. And, even science now knows that matter and energy come out of empty space. That's when creation starts; life follows naturally from creation because creation consists of nature with consciousness, awareness.

AMOS

It's almost as if consciousness wants to express itself. Look at the continuous creation all around us. Mike's wagon is full of the produce that grew just this season. It's all created.

MIKE

Once life is a given, it keeps on going. It doesn't matter if we are talking about people or horses or vegetables. I think we are getting more into the field of philosophy than wisdom. My ideas are subject to change; I've found out in the last few weeks talking to you guys.

THE GUNAS IN HUMAN BEINGS:

ANDY

How do human beings reflect the gunas? I made up a chart using the three gunas to describe seven types of people; the charts use a different description for the gunas that may mean more for the modern student:

PERSON TYPE	AVOIDS OR GRASPS: CAUSES CHANGE (ACTIVE)	RESISTS CHANGE (INERTIA)	ACCEPTS CHANGE (PURITY)
1	Primary	Secondary	Limited
2	Primary	Limited	Secondary
3	Secondary	Primary	Limited
4	Secondary	Limited	Primary
5	Limited	Primary	Secondary
6	Limited	Secondary	Primary
7	Balanced	Balanced	Balanced

I suppose that what we eat and how we exercise, even our posture affects the type we fall under in the chart. If we are constantly acting and moving our lives will be chaotic and difficult to manage; but, this is a good description of how human beings operate. The mind/body is always in a swarm of motion that just keeps on going and mutating as we go through the stages of life.

AMOS

The purity idea in the chart reminds me of one of the priests I know and of the lives of some of the saints that I read about.

MIKE

My horse is obviously part of nature. She would, perhaps, have inertia as primary, active as secondary and purity as limited. Or, active could be primary.

ANDY

Can the gunas be transcended? Our consciousness is colored by our nature. As we develop and conquer our conditioning we move towards the ideal of purity as the primary part of our nature. But, our (upper) Self has always been beyond the gunas. The Gita also **says the wise are not born again. Pure consciousness is the father, regardless of the womb.**

AMOS

I understand what you're saying but I don't think I could just let go and let my body/mind operate in any way its conditioning moves it. I sometimes resist eating and drinking sometimes. Maybe my resistance is also some kind of conditioning?

MIKE

I think that's the point. The body/mind is already doing its thing. Our conditioning is already dominant. It is going to stay that way until it changes, and then it will follow its new conditioning. If the (upper) self can somehow take over then we will be truly free. I see a conflict between the selves: It's a little like schizophrenia: two selves in the same space. In any event recognizing our conditioning will, I'm sure, change our lives and make authentic choices, at least, possible.

VITTORIO

Things keep coming; people are born and die; food grows; things don't change very fast. We keep what's ours, whatever we can get; we can get plenty.

Hey Amos. They've cut up a horse that died in the basement of the barn. They wrapped up his head for you. I want you to put it in the back seat of Marsony's car tonight so he finds it tomorrow. It's just a little joke between us, cabish?

OK, Vittorio. I don't like to get blood on my clothes; it reminds me of the war; I'll do it.

CHAPTER FOURTEEN:

TO EVOLVE, WE MUST LET GO OF OUR CIRCUMSTANCES.

Foreword: The tree of material existence can be felled with the axe of detachment letting one gain a viewpoint that transcends his physical existence.

MIKE

Hey Vittorio, here's the conversation we had today:

BEING DETACHED:

ANDY

How can we be detached? Being detached is something we must habituate to break our old habits of avoiding things we don't like and indulging in things we are attracted to. We must not let fear drive us unconscious of the possibilities for being human. If we are afraid of, for example, authority figures we should get closer to them and pay close attention to the reaction of the body/mind. Look at sensations, thoughts, attitudes and interpretations. Notice if you are blaming whoever you are involved with.

AMOS

I think there are things we should fear and avoid, such as bombs going off nearby or cars speeding down the street. We need to protect the body to maintain its usefulness; I wish I knew how to protect my mind. It would be good to notice how fear manifests in our body. If we could do it in wartime we could do it anywhere.

MIKE

I often get fear when the police are around. I'm afraid of getting arrested. I suspect that they may notice my fear and stop me when they notice. I'll have to get more involved with the police and see what that fear consists of.

AVOIDING REBIRTH:

ANDY

How can we avoid rebirth? This was a common problem discussed by meditators in the old books. One of the problems discussing this is that we are often reborn even during this life. It happens when we go through major changes in life: marriage, new job, death in a family, and many more. When these kinds of changes happen, and they always do, part of our conditioning loses its usefulness, and then we need to develop new conditioning so we will be efficient in the new situation. The implication of this question refers to the possibility of purification of the self by the Self. We go through a kind of rebirth with every significant change in life; they're like dying: losing a job, a relative dying, divorce, giving up a drug or alcohol addiction, graduating from school, and many other transitions that often are personal with each individual.

AMOS

I didn't know what I was doing at first when I went into the army, and I am having trouble now after getting out of the army. I feel terrible all she time. I still dream about the destruction I saw in Europe.

MIKE

I haven't had to make many changes in my life lately, but when I went to jail the last time for vagrancy it was a little difficult. In jail there is not a lot to do so you get used to it quickly. When I came out it took a while to get into the groove. Vittorio was a big help to me, setting me up with the horse and wagon and the produce route. Now I help him whenever he wants something. The Don gets whatever he wants.

ACTION AND PERCEPTION:

ANDY

Can consciousness affect action and perception? Remember the chart of the seven types of people? That represents seven ways that our nature is "colored." We very rarely experience consciousness in its purity. Some of us are running around all the time; some of us are sitting around all the time; some of us are detached and pure. Each of those types has its typical approach to action and perception. But consciousness or the Self can override our conditioned responses at times and lead us to freedom.

AMOS

I hope that if we eat the right food and do the right exercises we can change our nature. I flinch every time I hear a loud noise. I'll have to go to the Fourth of July celebration at Soldiers Field to watch my jumpiness and see if I can influence it. At least I'll test my commitment to stay instead or running.

MIKE

I hope that doing selfless service, meditating and eating fresh fruits and vegetables moves me in the right direction. I'm committed to doing just that. Vittorio says I can help with the collections at Mother Cabrini Church this Sunday. I'll have to buy something to wear. I haven't been to church for a long time. I hate to shop for and chose clothes.

CHARACTERISTICS IN CONSCIOUSNESS:

ANDY

Does consciousness bring characteristics with it when being reborn? When we go into a new phase of life here, like a new job, it does. We carry our existing nature to the new job. It works the same way during reincarnation after physical death. Consciousness, itself, is pure but when emerging into a baby it probably brings some conditioning with it that needs to be transcended to gain freedom. There are certainly some characteristics relating to the baby's parents that are a starting point. And, the parents do a lot of training (conditioning) of the baby as it grows up. The baby is also conditioned by surviving the birth process.

AMOS

I was jittery in the foxholes and I am jittery now after making the transition to civilian life. I remember being anxious before I joined the army as well.

MIKE

I seem to be the same for my whole life. Jail didn't change me. Since I got the horse and wagon business I seemed to mellow out some. Bringing fruits and vegetables to poor neighborhoods and seeing these poor people worrying about spending their coins, does something to you.

CONSCIOUS ENJOYMENT:

ANDY

Does consciousness enjoy sense objects? Consciousness lives through perceptions. It is the knower, or at least the carrier of Awareness. I think that consciousness is unattached to sense objects. Enjoyment is just one more kind of conditioning, and it's not consciousness that's conditioned, it's the ego.

AMOS

If the Self is the enjoyer, does it also find aspects of life that it doesn't like? I can answer my own question: The Self sees all this with the same way that we watch a movie. The drama is entertaining with sad stories, comedies, death and destruction, etc. You're right; it's the ego that has "feelings."

MIKE

We sure have plenty of drama in our lives. People are getting arrested, getting rich, committing suicide, murdering each other, using drugs, having accidents of all kinds, not getting what they want or need, getting what they don't want, living in fear, trapped with their bad habits, etc. This life is full of conflict caused by habits and conditioning: ours and others.

UNIVERSAL SELF:

. ANDY

Can we see the Self in others? The Self is not visible. When we notice someone doing selfless service that is the Self in operation. When we see someone fighting against their negative conditioning, that is the Self fighting.

AMOS

You're saying that the Self cannot be perceived, but you can know its operations.

MIKE

The Self can be known in some of the nuns that teach grammar school. It is not always present, but when you are in a class, the Self operates from time to time. When the nun is angry, the Self seems to hide, or maybe that's just me.

MEMORY IN CONSCIOUSNESS:

ANDY

How does consciousness bring the person to know and remember? Consciousness is the witness to all thoughts and perceptions. It is the only knower of experience. The ego remembers. When a memory is brought up, consciousness perceives it. Consciousness exists only in the "now" since it is eternal (out of time) and always pure. The Gita says that **memory, wisdom and discrimination owe their origins to consciousness.** I can see that without consciousness, there would be no perceptions to remember. The *Yoga Sutras* explain that there are five types of knowledge and they appear as patterns on consciousness that are observed by awareness. They are: right knowledge, wrong knowledge, conceptualization, sleep and memory. Since consciousness doesn't die, these patterns must show up again in another life.

AMOS

I wish some of my memories would not keep coming up. I guess I'm the main character in my life story, my "drama." And then I always try to explain or justify what happened, and characterize it by like/dislike/neutral.

MIKE

No matter what kind of life we lead, consciousness is the knower or witness. When we are conscious it is consciousness that is involved.

RELIGIOUS SCRIPTURES:

ANDY

Do all religious scriptures lead to consciousness? Religious scriptures all lead to a life of purity. Purity leads to bringing consciousness to the forefront. The scriptures were written by the pure. All paths lead to realization.

AMOS

There was a lot of praying in the foxholes. I think we were much more aware of our perceptions. We could tell how far away the bombs were by the way they sounded and how the ground shook.

MIKE

The catechism taught a children's form of purity. I'm not so sure that was a good way to start. I don't agree with much of those ideas now. I wouldn't dream of going to confession for swearing today. I think the church was just training (conditioning) us to get used to going to confession.

THE UPPER AND LOWER SELF:

ANDY

What is the difference between the self, the Self and Awareness?
I learned in the Theosophical Society Library that Awareness is like a light that shines through everything, without exceptions: people, rocks, clouds, empty space, oceans, vegetables, etc. It has no bias; nothing can affect it. The Self is pure consciousness, uncontaminated by any of its contents; and everything **is** its contents down to atoms and electrons and space. The self, the ego, the apparent self, the illusory self, are all composed of nature, the three gunas: activity, inertia, and purity. They appear to be alive, but they operate in a conditioned reactive mode only. They are the content of pure consciousness. There is no knower in the self. It is informed by consciousness; but it does remember (record events and ideas).

AMOS

So, if I understand this, Awareness is the source of consciousness, and then my conditioning leads me to have a false sense of "I." The conditioning has to be overcome to gain freedom.

MIKE

My horse has consciousness, but it may not have a strong sense of "I." She knows she is a horse when she's in heat. She must have her own conditioning; it's just different from a human being, or even from another horse. But, human beings are different from each other as well. We don't want to give a horse credit for operating in the same mode as human beings, but it does: it's all stimulus-response.

VITTORIO

God is everything that is; and is not; we are all God, or at least part of God: perhaps Angels; the best of us and the worst of us; we can do what we want while we are here on earth. The Mafia has always known this.

Hey Amos: that horse head did the trick. I think he'll be more forthcoming now, thanks.

CHAPTER FIFTEEN:

WE ALL HAVE THE ABILITY TO EVOLVE SPIRITUALLY.

Foreword: The human traits of divine and demonic natures; give up lust, anger, greed and discern between right/wrong using Buddhi (which is the human ability to maintain values) and hints from the scriptures.

MIKE

Hey Vittorio, here's what we talked about:

DEDICATION:

ANDY

Can we stay dedicated to the spiritual life? It takes determination and commitment. It requires action: meditation, proper exercise and nutrition, and the study of yoga, preferably as part of a group practicing in a tradition.

AMOS

I think that luck must enter into it. First we have to hear about it. Then noticing that there is a lot of suffering in life provides motivation to search for answers. Suffering is caused by the conditioning of us and others; when we know this our motivation is increased.

MIKE

I think the pool table analogy is a good one. We keep getting into trouble until we notice something that helps. Eventually we discover that there is a path that works well for us. Then we begin to purify our bodies and minds and gradually pull out of the morass of life. It is a great help if we discover some books that we can relate to, but a study group is a good step up. An expert teacher would be best. I think I'll go out to the Theosophical Society and join. That will get me a lot of good books to read and perhaps get some tips on finding a teacher.

SERVICE:

ANDY

Is there a best way to serve others? We only need to stay conscious in our lives and we will see what needs to be done. If we act with compassion and stay involved with others, we will be of help to them and also help ourselves. We help ourselves because when we serve others, our conditioning becomes obvious, and so does theirs. We are just God bringing God to God.

AMOS

I can support that idea. When I decided to serve my country I felt like it was a noble deed. I was full of patriotism and vigor. I didn't realize that we would be waking up early, training hard and cleaning toilets. There were a lot of things that I hated to do. Looking back I realize that type of work was good training. It destroyed a lot of my negative conditioning that started early in life.

MIKE

I see the same thing in the work that I do. There are a lot of people that I can hardly stand to be around. I have to serve them just like all the others. I'm beginning to see how my feelings were habituated since childhood. I can't stand to run into people that remind me of my father. Luckily, that doesn't happen too often. My customers have been mostly women; the men were all in the army.

SPIRITUAL QUALITIES:

ANDY

What qualities help on the spiritual path? I think being studious, and having a good heart or being compassionate are important. Leading a good life and staying healthy are also part of it.

AMOS

Knowing that life is full of suffering and looking for a way to avoid it is also a good start.

MIKE

I think being compassionate and having a good diet are important.

FREEDOM AND BONDAGE:

ANDY

What qualities lead to freedom and what to bondage? Finding out that you are trapped in your habits and conditioning is a big step. The Sufi's have a saying-you can't break out of jail until you know that you are in jail. Therefore, learn about the parameters of your individual jail; what do you habitually avoid or desire?

AMOS

I have a list: be fearless, committed to studying wisdom books, self controlled, truthful, gentle, compassionate and loving, detached. Also it is good to avoid anger, hypocrisy, malice and pride.

MIKE

I think joining a study group is a terrific start. My eyes have been opened.

LUST AND ANGER:

ANDY

Do lust, anger and greed lead to bondage? To me it seems obvious; they do.

AMOS

Lust and anger affects your physical health. When physical health is poor, mental and emotional health will also be poor.

MIKE

Once you start down that slide it's very difficult to turn things around. Very few fat people are out buying fruit and vegetables from my wagon.

GUIDES TO FREEDOM:

ANDY

Are the scriptures a good guide to freedom? Some scriptures are helpful to start one on the way to freedom. They all help to some extent. I think once we are on the path, our intuition will help us select appropriate scriptures.

AMOS

The Gita is an ancient book from the Hindu religion. There are not many similar books in the Christian religion.

MIKE

I think some of the writings of Saint Theresa of Avila or Saint John of the Cross are helpful.

VITTORIO

We give things up; we figure things out; we do selfless service; what's in a person's heart is important.

In the mafia we are always doing things that we would not do as individuals; this makes us aware of our conditioning (our likes and dislikes): doing things that we don't want to do. Then we can change our hearts; we have to. A good heart is necessary for clarity and appropriate action.

Hey, Amos, do you have a "good" heart?

I'm not connected with my heart or my feelings they way a lot of people are. The war left me without anything but anxiety fear and anger. When you have fear all the time you don't notice any other feelings. It puts you on high alert; you're always ready to fight or run. The only time I feel OK is when I'm in church; it relaxes me.

CHAPTER SIXTEEN:

WE MUST GIVE UP ALL OUR ATTACHMENTS IN LIFE.

Foreword: The three divisions of faith, thoughts, deeds and even eating habits corresponding to the three natures identifies the human traits of the divine (Satvic) and the demonic (Tamasic/Rajasic) natures. The Gita counsels that to attain the supreme destination one must give up lust, anger, and greed, and discern between right and wrong action by discernment through our developed sense of values (buddhi) and evidence from the scriptures.

MIKE

Hey Vittorio, here's what we talked about:

FAITH FROM BIRTH:

ANDY

How does our birth affect our faith? If we look at the three natures people have: active, inactive or pure we find the faiths they practice correspond to their natures. The pure worship the forms of God; the active worship power and wealth; the inactive worship spirits and ghosts. This is the chart we looked at before:

PURE	ACTIVE	INERTIA
Worship forms of God	Worship power and wealth	Worship spirits and ghosts
Food is mild, tasty, substantial, agreeable, nourishing	Food is salty or bitter, hot sour or spicy	Food is overcooked, stale, leftover and impure
Sacrifice with purpose	Sacrifice for show	Sacrifice ignoring the letter and spirit
Disciplines with faith unattached to results	Disciplines for respect and admiration	Disciplines to gain power or self torture
Worthy giving at the right time and circumstances	Giving with regrets or expectations	Inappropriate giving wrong circumstances
Accepts change	Avoids or grasps change	Resists change

Depending on the family that we are born into, we may start out as any combination of those: the seven types of human beings. If we eat the right food and make an effort, we will make progress. The problem is that we have to first hear about this possibility.

AMOS

So we are born into a situation that may not be optimal. I think we can be born again, even in this life. It may take a lot of purification, physical, mental, and emotional.

MIKE

Eating the right foods is a big step to move in the direction of purity. This action gives the message to the ego that we are serious about our lives.

WORSHIPING:

ANDY

From the chart we see that worshiping power and wealth or spirits and ghosts move us away from the pure nature that will help us gain freedom.

AMOS

It seems to me that worshiping power and wealth is where the mafia is at as well as some of our politicians and police. The country is all about worshiping power; think about the destruction of the Indians and the Buffalo and the other wars we have been involved in.

MIKE

Well I'm sure not worshiping wealth by selling fruit and vegetables from my wagon. Hang on; I am making a lot of money by my connection with Vittorio. But, Vittorio no longer cares about money; he is just keeping score and following orders and communicating to his bosses.

KINDNESS:

ANDY

The Gita advises that **we should practice austerity of mind through serenity, kindness, silence, self-control and purity.** A good meditation practice is the best start. Even better is hatha yoga and pranayama combined with meditation.

AMOS

During the war, different from what is commonly thought, there was a lot of being silent.

MIKE

I get a lot of serenity riding my wagon early in the morning, watching the sun come up.

FAITH AND NATURE:

ANDY

Here's a line from the Gita that I have trouble understanding: **The faith of every man conforms to his nature: Satvics worship forms of God; Rajasics worship power and wealth; Tamasics worship spirits and ghosts.**

AMOS

I think this refers to our beliefs. If we believe purity is good, we will become more pure. If we love to eat, we will be on the lookout for new kinds of food.

MIKE

It sounds like a religious idea. The Baptists say that if you believe in Christ, you will be saved. I guess this belief will make you a Christian. So our beliefs make us.

VITTORIO

If we know God we do what is best; that's why the mafia emphasizes going to church and especially doing the rosary. The sound of the prayers in Latin helps us change our hearts for the better. Helping collect the money during mass keeps us unattached to money. The mafia's point-of-view is we use money to keep score and to do good.

CHAPTER SEVENTEEN:

GIVE UP OUR HABITS AND CONDITIONING TO BE FREE.

(Acceptance)

Foreword: This chapter summarizes the conclusions of the previous seventeen chapters; give up all forms of dharma and surrender to consciousness. When we learn that all this is that (consciousness), we know God. When we can do that it puts our thinking/feeling ego into perspective: we don't take thoughts as being serious. But, we still have to watch out for cars when crossing the street. Maybe, when we are purified more, crossing the street will not be a problem.

MIKE

Hey Vittorio, I think I see what's being pointed to here. Here's what we talked about:

GIVING UP ACTIONS:

ANDY

What kind of renunciation should we perform? We should give up expectations of rewards for our acts. We should also **give up actions that spring from desires.**

The Gita adds: **To avoid an action through fear of physical suffering, because it is likely to be painful, is to act from passion, and the benefit of renunciation will not follow. He who performs an obligatory action, because he believes it to be a duty which ought to be done, without any personal desire to do the act or to receive any return – such renunciation is Pure.**

AMOS

I think we need to make a list first. We aren't conscious of our desires and fears. We know our fears when bombs are going off, but we have unknown fears left over from childhood that are no longer conscious. I have a fear of authority figures from when my Father would come home drunk and beat my Mother until she ran out into the street screaming.

MIKE

I can even see young kids that come to my wagon with a lot of strange characteristics that must be a result of fears. Some of them won't look you at you when asking for something. Maybe they see me as an authority figure. I seem powerful when they have to look up at me; and I also give them free fruit and they are usually hungry.

SELF SACRIFICE:

ANDY

Self sacrifice and giving are purifying. By self sacrifice it means giving up our "strange" characteristics: upsets, fears and strong desires. We first have to do some self examination to know what they are. They are what has biased our character. Giving money to the poor or helping them brings us to know our driving sensations, our motivations. Our resistance will show up because it is automatic. If we start out in this direction, we will soon find the thoughts and feelings that are driving us. If we find them then we can deal with them by seeing how they have been habituated.

The Gita adds: **Relinquishment is distinguished from renunciation. The sages say that renunciation means forgoing an action which springs from desire; and relinquishing means the surrender of the results of action: accepting whatever comes from doing your work, the fruit.** To give up actions that spring from desire, we must first know what our unconscious desires and fears are. We must know our beliefs. **We know that everything comes from this earth and goes back into the earth.**

AMOS

After joining the army I found out that I really liked to sleep late and take it easy after meals. I didn't like physical work. I had to give up these things I didn't like and give them up quickly. I'm a better person for it; I now stand up straight. After spending time around bombs going off, I find I'm afraid of noises. I jump. At least that is a fear that I know. I see what you mean about coming from the earth. That's a saying from the bible. This is always changing.

MIKE

I've been easy going all my life. Maybe I should get a job as a laborer? I do make a practice of giving away some of my produce to people and kids that look like they need it. That sometimes brings up funny feelings in me. Maybe I'll try giving away produce to some people that don't seem to need it and see what kinds of sensations and thoughts come up? When something is always changing it reminds me of the waves on Lake Michigan.

PLANS AND EXPECTATIONS:

ANDY

Is planning and expectation a problem? Some of our planning is automatic. I have made a habit of finding something that needs correcting in most of the situations in life.

AMOS

I expected my army service to be all about shooting guns and getting medals. Was I disappointed! Looking back, most of my service didn't meet my expectations, and it gave me time to grow up.

MIKE

Most of the plans that I am conscious of seem to work OK. My work with the produce is good; my work with Vittorio is good. In the beginning I didn't know how much time I would have to spend taking care of the horse and the wagon. I didn't like waking up at 4:30 every morning either. I got over it. Now I suspect that I have other habitual plans that are not conscious. I'll have to try to make a list.

- When I was just a kid, I decided that school wasn't important for me. Now I know that I'm pretty smart and I should have stayed in school through high school. I guess I planned to quit, because I didn't like some of the teachers.

- I guess I always plan to avoid the things I don't like.

PLEASANT AND UNPLEASANT WORK:

ANDY

How should we do our work if it is pleasant or unpleasant? I think we should do all our work without expectations of rewards, indifferent to results but doing our best. When we are doing the work expected of us we are acting on purpose and exerting our influence on nature. The Gita also says: **When a man has no sentiment and no personal vanity, when he possesses courage and confidence, cares not (don't give a shit) whether he succeeds or fails, then his action arises from Purity.**

AMOS

I remember, in the army, we were encouraged to work for rewards and to avoid punishment. We were judged on how we dressed and how we made our beds and cleaned our guns, and a lot of other things. That's how they trained you. And sometimes, when I really went all out for a long time, I no longer cared.

MIKE

I see what you mean. If I have to clean out the wagons greasy axels or treat a sick horse, I don't like it. I almost get sick to my stomach, but I do it anyway.

INCENTIVES TO ACTION:

ANDY

The Gita declares: **Knowledge, the knower and the object of knowledge, these are the three incentives to action; and the act, the actor and the instrument are the threefold constituent.** The knower of action is pure awareness. The object of knowledge must be experience as opposed to conceptual knowledge. The actor, we have learned, is nature, the gunas. The actor might be consciousness again. I'm not sure. When we are acting on purpose it seems different from when we react to some stimulus. If we choose to go to school and study engineering, for instance, it is like laying new track for the railroad. It will change our view of the life to come. It doesn't mean that we will like the life we get.

AMOS

Since we are all conditioned, what is the requirement for the godhead? How is the godhead involved? Is it more than **the witness, pure awareness**?

MIKE

My horse is performing actions all the time. It's hard to see divine will except for the fact that all of existence must involve divine will. This is all consciousness, and possibly everything together can be considered the divine will. Any action requires all the rest of the cosmos to operate in.

WE ARE PART OF NATURE:

ANDY

Are all of us just part of nature? The key notion here is "part." By nature is meant the three qualities, or gunas: motion, resistance, and purity. Everything that exists has those three qualities. Those qualities come from pure consciousness.

AMOS

When I think of the tragedies around the world, the sick and starving people, the dictators stealing the wealth of some countries and the wars, I don't know how this could be considered anything but conditioned nature doing its thing, running on automatic pilot. It's difficult to call any of this a sin. Even language starts to lose its meaning.

MIKE

I agree. The divine will may change things, from time to time, but then conditioning goes on, with more changes. There is still conflict, different than it would have been. If we gain freedom, we can be an influence for the good, but I doubt it. There have been a lot of great saints and they seem to have been offset by great sinners. This is all just nature doing its thing. The pool game is a good analogy. We can see things as conflict or just as life going on with success and failure and drama, lots of drama.

THE SELF IN ALL BEINGS:

ANDY

When we are pure we see the (upper) Self in all beings and we work without attachment. When we are dominated by activity we see separate beings and are motivated by desire. When we are dominated by inactivity we mistake a small part for the whole and work without considerations. It seems to me that I have been recently dominated by purity because I'm always reading and studying, but I still get involved in the world. I think that Amos has been dominated by activity out of necessity due to being in the war. Mike I'm not sure of; he may be dominated by inactivity, but I don't think so.

AMOS

I'm so active that I'm shaky from anxiety. I have trouble thinking straight; my mind is in a whirl of activity.

MIKE

I think we should watch the people that come to buy from the wagon and see if we can identify what quality dominates their lives. It would be a good exercise.

LIFE CHARACTARISTICS:

ANDY

After watching people all day we found the following characteristics:

Pure	Active	Inactive
Clean	Messy	Dirty
Alert	Excited	Dull
Good posture	Jittery	Slump
Clear requests	Thin, can't decide	Fat, slow making up the mind

THE GITA SAYS THIS IS HOW THINGS WORK:

QUALITY			
	PURE	ACTIVE	INACTIVE
Right and Wrong, Freedom and Bondage	Understands	Confused	Reverses
Will Power	Leads to Harmony	Supports Greed	Lacking
Happiness comes from	Sustained Effort brings Joy	Pleasures bring misery	Sleep and Intoxication

Responsible for	Self Control and a Pure Heart	Trade and Agriculture	Service
Justifications and Rational for Actions	Free from Error	Mistakes Made	Inaccurate

I think that I understand right and wrong, but that is more due to being raised in a Catholic grammar school. I understand the words that are taught here, but more is implied than words can teach. The Gita also teaches that reason and conviction are threefold, according to the Quality which is dominant. And, there is nothing anywhere on earth or in the higher worlds which is free from the three Qualities. Don't expect to be free when you go to heaven.

AMOS

I guess I'm active because I'm jittery most of the time. But this study group is helping me to be more relaxed, even when I'm jittery. I guess you could say that I'm relaxed about being jittery. This is no heaven.

MIKE

I'm not jittery, but I guess I'm pretty inactive. I just sit around most of the time, but my posture is good and I'm alert. It is hard for me to define myself. But, now that I think about it, those characteristics only apply to these body/minds; and that's not who we are. This is hard to keep straight or even discuss.

ANDY

I can see why some of us are attracted to sustained effort. I think you are like that, Mike, but sometimes we are one and sometimes we are another. The balance of those qualities is always changing.

AMOS

I saw all kinds of people in the army. They were mostly active, but there were a lot of drunks. Some of the officers were intellectuals. A lot of us liked to sleep or withdraw into depression.

MIKE

At the South Water Market there are a lot of skinny, active people loading trucks. There aren't many heavy drinkers. In the mafia there are all types. My customers are all types: some are fat, some read a lot, and some are skinny. The housewives read and daydream a lot; their husbands are still away in the army or died in service.

ANDY

I can see the need for keeping a pure heart. I have always watched my thoughts to avoid my automatic criticism of others. I discovered this automatic reaction so I stopped; I might have the thought, but I didn't express it.

AMOS

I don't understand the responsibility aspect of being human. This division must have come from antiquity. I interpret this as saying that all or most of us in the army had inactive natures. Maybe the army structure forced these, normally inactive, people to be active, changing their natures.

MIKE

I guess this fits the South Water Market. It is a very active place responsible for trade and agriculture.

RESPONSIBILITIES:

ANDY

When we consider our natural responsibilities, can we change what we are responsible for; can we change our nature? I think if we become free of our conditioning or get familiar with it, we can transcend our nature. We can let it continue as is, we can act in spite of it, we can develop new conditioning or habits, or we can override it when necessary. The Gita also adds: **It is better to do one's own duty, however defective it may be, than to follow the duty of another.** I guess this means that we don't have to change; if we do change, then just accept our new self.

AMOS

I guess that means that whatever our nature, we should focus on getting free of our conditioning, or at least recognizing it. That means following the earlier instructions on yoga. When we start to discover our conditioning, that means that we have already changed; just keep accepting it.

MIKE

When we follow our natures, we reduce the stress we might otherwise incur. There is some stress from being mindful enough to notice the automatic reactions we all have when responding to our environments until we make being mindful a part of our conditioning. When we get to that point we can do as we like; the important part is watching our mind's interpretation of life. I can accept that.

PERFECTION:

ANDY

Can everyone attain perfection? I think it is possible for most of us. We have to be willing to do what is required. We should know that consciousness is already perfect; it accepts anything: what we consider good, evil or otherwise.

AMOS

When you think about it most people will not even hear about this. And if you consider many who have heard about it, not many of those will pursue the opportunity to study and practice enough to be successful in one lifetime.

MIKE

Don't forget that there are a lot of people that are not very intelligent or have some mental illness or sever physical problems. I suspect that a "master" could make an impact, even on those with serious problems.

SUPREME PERFECTION:

ANDY

What is the supreme perfection? Who we are is already in union with God. Going beyond that is seeing that what we are, pure awareness, is the cause and support of God, as well as space, time and everything else in the universe. I wonder how I know all this.

AMOS

We may be God, but we don't consciously know it. It's like being wealthy, but losing our memory and not remembering we are wealthy.

MIKE

I feel happy just hearing about it. What could be better?

LIKES AND DISLIKES:

ANDY

Can discrimination or knowing our likes and dislikes be free from error? I think there is a progression from the very gross reactions to the subtle. If we work on the gross first, and take some of the energy out of them, we will get more and more accurate, eventually able to discern even the most subtle. After a time we realize that all minds are, in some ways "insane." Experiential learning becomes very important, because that is the only way we can each find out our likes and dislikes or our fears or any conditioned motivation. Experiential learning is non-verbal; consider for example, how we know how to walk or ride a bike. What we like or dislike is experiential.

AMOS

When we do it like that it seems to me that there is no chance of failure. We just keep on going, even though we don't like what we are doing. It's like the army that way. And we will keep reacting in strange ways until we don't. At any particular time we may be upset about something or be strongly attracted to some women because of her shape or how she's dressed. There are all kinds of stuff that motivates us, and it's all our personal conditioning.

MIKE

That's how life works: we just keep on going. When we run into this kind of opportunity and see what it can mean, we go with the flow and pursue it.

THE QUIET LIFE:

ANDY

Should we lead a quiet life in order to be successful? I think that it would be good to go on a retreat from time to time. All the great teachers seem to recommend this.

AMOS

When you have spent five years in the war, a retreat seems like a good idea. But normal life is looking pretty good to me as well even though I am usually pretty anxious.

MIKE

I feel like I'm always on a retreat. Waking up early, hooking up my horse and wagon, driving slowly to the market, buying produce, driving slowly back to the neighborhoods, selling produce to people I don't know very well. The whole day is spent being pretty detached. But even then I notice small aggravations. It's usually so quiet that the tricks of my mind are easily noticeable now that I'm on my toes and watching.

GOD LEADS:

ANDY

Is God leading us around with opportunities and thoughts? I think, what is meant here by "us" is the body/mind. The body/mind is part of nature and is not an "us." Opportunities and thoughts are also part of nature. But, nature is part of God as well, so it is just God leading God. Hey Mike: this morning I was watching God pulling God through God. And you thought you were just driving your horse and wagon down the street-think again.

AMOS

So during the war we were just God battling God? I see it, but that was not what I thought at the time. Joe Louis said: "we are on God's side;" that was true, and so was everyone else; the Germans, Japanese and Italians had the same thought.

MIKE

Giddiyup, Goddamnit.

WORSHIPING GOD:

ANDY

Worshiping God at any level or in any form implies some kind of sacrifice. Traditionally time, money, effort and allegiance are part of worship. Study and attention is also an important part. There are many smaller gods: war, money, power, love, sex... The ancient Greeks understood this very well.

AMOS

Well this and other countries sure worship war. War must be God's work.

MIKE

All work is God's work. Me selling produce, the Mafia selling heroin, prostitutes turning tricks: it's all God working with God. This is all one thing and we call it God when we start to see the truth.

WORSHIPING GODS:

ANDY

Should we worship god(s)? I think it is a good thing, but how it is done will depend on where we are in life. When you see all this as one God, worship will be different than if you have just made your first communion. It's different for different levels of consciousness. But, I think that any kind of worship is training for worship (the mind paying attention to) of consciousness.

AMOS

What you worship is what you get. Worshiping war gets you war; worshiping money gets you money; Worshiping heroin gets you heroin.

MIKE

Most of the time what I see is my horse, my customers, and Vittorio. I get them. I'm not worshiping my horse's ass, but now that I think about it Vittorio gets my attention whenever he wants it.

THE SOUL:

ANDY

What is a Self or Soul? When we talk about our "higher" Self or Soul we are talking about the source of divine will. Most of the time, our body/ mind is on automatic pilot that depends on our conditioning. Our Soul can override the normal tendencies and take us in a new direction. We just have to be alert to the normal workings of the mind and its desires. Even the Christian bible says "the mind is exceedingly wicked." They had that right.

AMOS

Sometimes we saw that happen in the war. When most of us were hiding in our foxholes a few others were doing heroic stuff: throwing hand grenades or using their rifles or crawling up on the enemy. That took a lot of willpower.

MIKE

I can even see that in my day-to-day operations. There are some people that I can hardly stand to wait on, but I grit my teeth and just keep going and keep my feelings to myself.

KARMA:

ANDY

What is karma? Karma is traditionally thought of as the Golden Rule: What you sow, so you will reap. A more accurate description is the actions or thoughts that have conditioned us. When thought through we see that it takes more than one life to balance everything out. Even in one lifetime we can see that the conditioning we have developed is carried with us as we change our circumstances. Often when we get our first job we realize that certain bosses make us very uncomfortable, or we have strong attractions to only some members of the opposite sex.

AMOS

I had to overcome a lot of that kind of stuff whenever I was assigned to a new sergeant. In Europe, any sex you could find was good sex. There were willing women everywhere because so many of the men had died or were missing. The young women, especially, had little hope of finding a man their own age.

MIKE

It makes me feel better to think of my negative feelings as being only leftover conditioning from my childhood. They are easier to resist when I think of them that way.

DHARMA:

ANDY

What is dharma? Dharma is a word from the Sanskrit that means to behave according to religious and social codes. In Buddhism it means the truth about the way things are and will always be. Sometimes it can mean behaving according to your nature. Human beings rarely do anything other than where their conditioning leads them until they meet some conflicting issue where they are forced to, or have the opportunity to, make a choice, and take a particular action. For the most part our choices follow our conditioning; we can "lay new track in life by making commitments. Some important ones have to do with being good, family, practicing Yoga or Buddhism or meditation.

AMOS

I get it. When you are in the army you follow the code; when you are in jail you follow the code. Things are different for single people and for married people, for children and for adults.

MIKE

Things have been different for me since Vittorio hired me. The mafia has its own code. Selling produce doesn't interfere with my mafia behavior. My work selling fruits and vegetables is quite different from my work for Vittorio; I owe my life to him.

MAYA:

ANDY

What is Maya? Maya means illusion. Life in this world is considered to have an illusory nature. One aspect is that we think we think we are in control our lives, while actually we are at the mercy of our conditioning and the circumstances we find ourselves in. Not many of us have even heard of a higher Self, let alone how conditioned we are. I found a list among my mother's stuff, and I made copies for all of us: it was titled:

A FEW ASPECTS OF MAYA

- We don't understand or know reality.

- We are conditioned beings in a conditioned universe.

- We never know what we will say until after we speak.

- This reality is all one interconnected thing.

- There is no such thing as "I," "me" or "mine."

- We do not control the mind; it is an independent operator.

- We do not control the body; it is constructed out of independent parts; we can only control specific actions when we are "on purpose;" the Self is present.

- We are an integral part of "God" and we don't know it.

- All this reality is "God:" eternal, consciousness, bliss.

- This is not "our" life or "my" life; there is only "the" life: consciousness or God in continual motion. Life on earth is all in a constant process of change, with nothing separate, like a wave is not separate from the ocean, senses, emotions, will, intellect, ego all are in flux; thoughts and opinions all change; who/what am I is the most important question that anyone can ask of themselves. The universe is a conscious body that we share with everyone and everything.

- We are all conditioned by the many roles we play in life and we don't know it. This is traditionally called **karma** which means action. All our thoughts and emotions are a result of past actions and decisions. This is hidden from us because we believe we are our minds and bodies instead of knowing or seeing we are consciousness. The notion of our inability to see this and to see that what we are is pure consciousness or awareness is defined as **maya**. Many Sanskrit words are used when trying to describe reality because they have no English equivalent.

- There is an authentic self, the Self, which is capable of making choices that change the future of the universe. However, the choices are limited by the presence of the existing reality. The Self is not bound by past actions; it can make choices about the current situation: if you want new scenery you must lay new track-the difference is only in the scenery or the kind of drama.

- When we say or think that the world exists, in our perceptions, the implication, usually not realized, is that the world is not absolute, pure consciousness, but is known by awareness. Pure consciousness and pure awareness are free of time and space. However, since the world is created out of consciousness, it is absolute, but we don't know it.

- It is like an image in a mirror: we may call it by its usual name, not using the word "image" but that will not be "true:" it is an image, only. The world of our perceptions is like that. When the great teachers say that all this is that, they mean that all our perceptions are actually pure consciousness, and they are pointing out the fact that we don't know it or see it that way.

- For most of us making a choice depends on perception, voice over, and action; these things depend on the role we are playing. If we don't have a strong commitment in our lives, we are on an automatic, directionless path that depends on our conditioning and what situations we run into. If we make a conscious, on purpose, commitment or promise we can change our conditioning, e.g. deciding to become a writer. We are still conditioned; we may not like the change, but we are laying new track.

- Freedom is seeing/accepting the separation between the Self (awareness) and nature (which also includes consciousness and what is ordinarily called "God"). Consciousness is a part of nature; it doesn't know itself.

- Change comes from history; just look around. Everything we see is a result of creation and action in the past, including our minds and bodies. And, it keeps coming as actions, ideas and new things. Consciousness has a tendency to manifest.

- Under the influence of Maya the various domains of knowledge are :

  o Perception which can be corrected

  o Inferences, when made properly, are connected by a universal law.

  o Verbal testimony is gained from texts such as the Vedas, but the literal interpretation is merely mind knowledge, and the mind cannot know the Self; it is of a different domain.

  o Comparison to previous knowledge that is known to be true.

  o Negation is the absence of the object.

  o The trio of knower, means and object

- One way to overcome the "I" feeling/role is to pay attention to the ongoing stream of "motivations" and see how they have an arbitrary nature. They are all part of one moving, changing "thing" that we call nature or "God."

- Because of the will to exist, these "powers" go on forever; new stuff, new thoughts, new roles, keep on coming.

- The past and future of an object is known, e.g. an apple lying on the ground in an apple orchard: seed, tree, flowering, pollination, fruit, fruit fall, decay, seed, ground, etc. The characteristics' of the past and future are known to have the characteristics' of the gunas, purity, motion and resistance; they tend to blur together; their proportions are constantly changing in any given object; our interpretations and point-of-view changes as well. This is all empty of inherent existence so we can be creative with our interpretations.

- Most phenomena's changes are microscopic and slow, like a rotting apple; this usually gives things a false sense of permanence or apparent existence, sometimes called dharma. All of reality is actually granular in nature, like the apple; space, time, gas, fire, liquid and earth are created out of a primordial granularity infused with awareness. They are sometimes called mind creations.

- Our everyday mental patterning (a rush of thoughts, feelings, reactions and perceptions) is so turbulent that reality is hidden; each pattern is conditioned by the previous pattern; the world is a clockwork reality, in this view, but each observer is affected differently by what they observe and how they interpret (good/bad/danger) and react. With mindfulness and experience it will be discovered that this mental patterning is a result of conditioning and therefore impersonal: not from any real self. These impulses can be resisted once they are recognized by using the will not to react and/or taking contrary actions; it may take some practice or commitment to develop this will.

- Patterns of consciousness are observed only by awareness and there are only five: right perception, misperception, conception, sleep and remembering.

- The kleshas are five: ignorance of the true nature of reality, egoism (being a self), desire, avoidance, and survival). They can be neutralized by tracing them back to their origin and observing them through contemplation, without automatically following the path of easiest reaction; then the kleshas disappear; reactive thoughts, emotions and actions cease. See examples of the truth process in the appendix for a technique of taking the energy out of strong fears.

- Suffering comes from a human tendency to misunderstand reality; sit up straight, relax, focus and keep returning to the present moment, practice stopping the mind for short times by counting the out breaths slowly, just so the "normal" onrush of thoughts can be noticed. This process provides a perspective on the ordinary thought process; most of us don't realize that our minds are constantly pushing thoughts and interpretations of what we perceive: the situations we are involved with.

- This is all one; conceptualizing this is of no use, just as conceptualizing water is of no help for being thirsty.

- Egoism is caused by an accumulation of the kleshas; it considers this accumulation as a self: "itself," and this sense of self stays "attached" through all changes and conditionings in this life and in the next.

- The body is habituated along with mental and emotional conditionings. Yoga has always addressed this aspect of maya with exercises (hatha). It's good to do body work, but without expectations, a regular practice, like brushing the teeth. If expectations are added, we will only change the nature of the habituation and make it more difficult to address. Rolfing and massage are also beneficial, perhaps more so because we are in the hands of a practitioner, and we do not know what is being addressed. The primary requirement for us is to remain mindful of whatever comes up in the any process we go through: reactions, thoughts and sensations that come up like a swarm.

- Realization is not an intellectual event; the mind has to remember the elements of practice and remain neutral while it moves towards stillness.

- Since awareness is not an entity, who/what is experiencing unsatisfactoriness, impermanence, selflessness, etc.? We can speculate that we could develop an ego to benefit humanity that would be born again and again in new bodies.

- The cloud of consciousness is all one thing that is seen and activated by awareness which is eternal and everywhere. Consciousness is empty of inherent existence itself, continually changing; although its nature may also be seen to be eternal: a granular cloud that has a tendency to vibrate, thereby starting time and space and a dharma stream empty of any self; it is an impersonal consciousness that, on the surface is in constant motion and, in the "depth" is unmoving, eternal and pure. It is sometimes referred to as Brahman or God.

- All things are, therefore, interconnected and impermanent.

- The Gita is a study of **knowing** and **being.**

- In spite of this being an illusion, maya, we love it and as consciousness we accept everything in it; the mind, however, goes through the **stages of dying** as it changes and moves towards acceptance.

Another way that we get mislead is after getting involved in some forms of yoga we learn about the subtle bodies, the *koshas* in Sanskrit. There are usually five discussed:

1. The food body: a wave from the earth.

2. The "air" body: a wave from the atmosphere.

3. The mind body: a wave from conditioning.

4. The wisdom body: a wave from insight into conditioning.

5. The bliss body: a wave from freedom.

The first thing to know about these bodies is that they are all part of nature, the gunas. Nevertheless they are worth cultivating because they are what we use in this life.

It also sometimes helps to differentiate between the states of consciousness:

- The waking state that looks outward
- The dreaming state which looks inward
- The deep sleep state which includes the casual body
- The transcendent state, pure consciousness, which is experienced between the transitions from one state to another and during meditation.

AMOS

I'm still getting used to the idea that this is all God acting on God, or you could say just as accurately, nature acting on nature, or emptiness acting on emptiness; God is everything, all this moving earth with its creatures, especially during wars. There is no truth to the notion of being "at cause" in our circumstances. When we play pool, for instance, we like to think that "our" skill has something to do with the results. However, our skill has to do with our physical attributes which are inherited. High scores also have to do with the skill of those that built or didn't build the tables and created the balls and cue sticks and the person that set them up. Also, as we have discussed there is no such thing as and "I." This is one of the primary illusions of Maya.

MIKE

I could say that I am responsible for the days produce sales. To do that I would have to ignore my horse, as well as the people that built the wagon, and their ancestors and opportunities. I couldn't drive my wagon down these streets if the streets hadn't been built by others. And, my customers don't materialize out of thin air. I need customers; I need farmers; I need trains. I'm glad we won the war or I would have a much different life. It's complicated.

DIET:

ANDY

Diet is important when trying to realize the truth of existence. Prohibition or prescription is a traditional part of many religions. There have always been prohibitions about what food to eat and what not to eat. Certainly staying healthy is important. But diet may help one to maintain, decrease or increase purity. It is also a signal to our body/mind that we are serious about, even worshiping, the path.

AMOS

In the army we ate what was served. Sometimes that was only "K" rations or canned franks and beans, or canned scrambled eggs warmed on a burner. The diet was designed to keep us active. We were so active we drank alcohol every chance we had, for balance or stress relief. Alcohol has a lot of purity as far as the guna interpretation goes. It is made from a process of purification.

MIKE

If all food is God's food, we don't have to worry about our diet. But we know if we eat too much pasta and sweets we will get fat. That's not healthy. I suspect that the traditions of what to eat or not are ancient knowledge that is being passed down.

MEDITATION TRADITIONS:

ANDY

The meditative traditions seem to be unique by including physical and breathing exercises in their traditions, as well as diet. When you consider our habitual conditioning developed over the course of a lifetime, you have to believe that this conditioning is programmed into the body. It takes place in terms of chronically stiff muscles, postures, facial expressions, weaknesses and strengths, and deteriorations and illnesses. Also, our breathing rate depends on our emotional reactions to the environment.

AMOS

When we were exposed to danger, we would often hold our breath for long times. Even things like being in a hurry or being anxious, changes the breath.

MIKE

Even my horse huffs at times.

POSITIONS IN LIFE:

ANDY

Why are the positions in life important? When we pass through the many stages of life we pick up different types of conditioning. Some types are reinforced and some are gradually dropped. We change conditioning when we get a new job or get married for instance. We do learn (get conditioned, form habits). Dropping our old conditioning is stressful. It's like part of us is dying. That's when most of us go through the stages of death: Denial, Anger, Bargaining, Depression and Acceptance. More often than not we get hung up at one of the stages.

AMOS

In the army I picked up the habit of eating regular meals. Before then I never had regular meals.

MIKE

Many of the people that buy from me that I don't like are the same kind of people that I had problems with since I was a baby. I had a fat aunt that was mean to me and now I feel angry whenever I see a fat woman.

VITTORIO

We don't have to follow our thoughts or feelings; they are just left over from growing up; what the church teaches is OK; what the Gita teaches is OK: we are OK no matter what

Following your orders in the Mafia makes you free and earns you a living. When I got into the Mafia and **accepted** their ways and become a made man, my depression went away. Maybe it will do the same for you, Amos?

It seems strange, but I know just what you mean. The experience of wrestling around with that bloody horse's head left me not caring about anything. That's freedom for me: don't fear anything; don't want anything; I have it all, except there is no "I."

CHAPTER EIGHTEEN:

SOMETIMES IT IS NECESSARY TO LEARN NEW APPROACHES TO ADVANCE ON THE PATH.

Foreword: When beginning on the path it is necessary to recondition the body/mind to make a habit out of the routine steps that are appropriate to make advances.

LISTS FOR LIFE:

ANDY

Making a list was a good idea, Mike. Here is mine:

- I always make sure that I have plenty of books around to read when there's nothing else to do.
- I don't like most grown up men; I have always avoided them. I'll have to find out what that's about.

AMOS

- I try to avoid loud noises; I get surprised often when I least expect it.

- I notice that I never miss these daily outings. That must take some planning that I didn't notice.

MIKE

I watched out for my mind planning things that I wasn't paying attention to and found these things:

- I don't even have to think about when I will run out of Muscatel, I automatically buy some, even before I need it.

- I plan to get what I want.

- I do the same with feed for the horse.

- I go to see Vittorio every day, that's a habit; is that the same as making a plan?

PLANNING FOR THE PATH:

ANDY

It seems like our minds do a lot of planning ahead that we are not conscious of. If we are going to stay on this path we need to make a list so we can reinforce the good habits and stop the bad habits and try things to see if we learn anything.

Here's a list that I made:

- Practice yoga: meditation, hatha, and pranayama (**be a yogi**).

- Experiment with sleep hours, diet and exercise (**be watchful of sensations**).

- Avoid cigarettes and alcohol and other addicting substances (**be healthy**).

- Study yoga (**be a yogi**), perhaps join the Theosophical Society (**be a Theosophist**).

- Join a meditation group to get training (**be a meditator**).

- Using the ability to "**be or not to be**" is the shortest way to doing what this is all about, I think. It takes study, and not just reading and memorizing the information in books.

- We need to study how we are in life and how our minds operate (**be mindful**).

- Since we have trouble keeping this information in our minds, the lists become critical (**be a list maker**). I say that the things that we avoid, the things that we are attracted to and the things that make us upset are extremely important.

AMOS

That list sounds like it's pretty complete. I would add:

- Volunteer for selfless service (**be useful**). I noticed that I'm not always sure about the outcome of my helping out: is it good or bad. My experience in the army made me very aware of that. I guess it's all about having a good heart and doing what you think is right at the time (**be good**).

- Watch and make notes about the tricks that our minds play on us (**be mindful**).

MIKE

- Give up Muscatel (quit **being an alcoholic.**)

- Take better care of my wagon (maintain your lifestyle: **be complete**).

- Help out my poorest customers (**be a giver**).

ADVAITA VEDANTA:

ANDY

The last time I went to the Theosophical Society, in Wheaton, I found that there was a Sunday evening meeting of an Advaita Vedanta group. "Advaita" refers to the identity of the true Self, **Atman**, and the highest Reality, **Brahman**, which is everything/no-thing and is also Pure Consciousness. Pure Consciousness appears to consist of a material granular reality that is infused with Pure Awareness as described in the Shambhala Dragon edition of the *Yoga Sutras*.

We are all invited to join. They study, do exercises and read from a book: *The Transparency of Things,* by Rupert Spira. Why don't we all go this Sunday and join the class?

AMOS

Sunday's good for me. I'm in.

MIKE

I don't do anything on Sunday evenings. I'll go. I can even drive. We'll even take my car instead of the horse and wagon.

APPENDIX ONE:
THE TRUTH PROCESS INSTRUCTIONS

The truth process can be used when trying to take the energy out of, for example, returning upsets. They are conditioned "emotional" stimulus-response reactions to and environmental condition. It works best if a regular practice of hatha yoga, pranayama and meditation is being followed.

1. Make a list of your recurring upsets.

2. Pick one to try.

3. Recall and actual time when the incident happened.

4. Go through the following list:

   a. When did it happen?

   b. Where did it happen?

   c. Who was there?

   d. What happened?

   e. How did you feel?

   f. What thoughts did you have?

   g. Go back to the beginning of the incident and see if you missed anything.

   h. Recall an earlier, similar incident.

   i. Go through the incident as above.

   j. This can be repeated and the chain can be followed through life and beyond, often to other lives.

APPENDIX TWO:
MEDITATION INSTRUCTIONS

1. Meditate in a quiet comfortable place.

2. Do some preliminary stretching exercises: conditioning is structured in the body.

3. Count the out breaths up to four, with a slight pause after each breath, and then start over.

4. When thoughts interfere, gently go back to the counting.

5. Maintain an attitude of restful alertness.

6. In the beginning do for five minutes twice a day before meals. During meditation the metabolism is moving to deeper levels of rest; this conflicts with the digestive process

7. The time can be extended to twenty minutes, when ready.

8. It is good to meditate in a group with an experienced teacher, if available; Transcendental Meditation, Shambhala Programs, and the Himalayan Institute have good programs.

Notes:

- Classical Yoga aims for complete thought suppression.

- As a meditative exercise Yoga is withdrawal from the particular and identification with the universal: contemplating the Self as Consciousness.

APPENDIX THREE:
BEING INSTRUCTIONS

Instructions for being have been used in religion since religions have started. Some examples are:

- From the Beatitudes: Blessed are ...

    o The poor in spirit-BE HUMBLE

    o Those who mourn-BE SAD

    o The meek-BE MEEK OR MILD MANNERED

    o Those who hunger for righteousness-BE RIGHT

    o The merciful-BE MERCIFUL

    o The pure in heart-BE GOOD

    o The peacemakers-BE PEACEFUL

    o Those who are persecuted for righteousness' sake-BE WILLING

The opportunity to be what we want is especially easy for children. Religions have always taken advantage of this propensity. If adults are interested in using this as a practice try one or more of these suggestions as possibilities:

- Be a yogi: develop a daily practice of hatha yoga, pranayama, and meditation.

- Be a theosophist: join the Theosophical Society in America and participate in some of their programs.

- Be an Advaita Vedantist: study the principles and join a group to advance knowledge.

- Be good; purify your heart. There are no particular instructions; you have to go within and use your intuition.

- Being instructions are instructions about modifying one's existence. As a comparison:

  o Advaita Vedanta is a so-called substance ontology. It holds that underneath all this moving multiplicity are unchanging and permanent entities.

  o Buddhism is a process ontology, and it holds that there exists nothing permanent and unchanging.

When I was young, my uncles used to ask me what I wanted to be when I grew up; they would prompt me with suggestions: policeman, fireman, etc. These were good jobs for Irish Catholics in Chicago in the thirty's and forty's.

Choosing to be something is a way to determine your conditioning, but don't expect the choice to make you happy. Being satisfied with the choice is the best you get; there is no "being happy." Happy is one of those nebulous conditions.

One precaution: Watch your tendency towards "greed." This is often trivialized as some think in terms of food or possessions. These things are important to consider, but there are also non-material issues. For example, don't be greedy to be a winner. This commitment will skew your life in undessirable ways.

APPENDIX FOUR:
THE SWARM:

Most of us know what a "swarm" is e.g. "a swarm of insects." We also recognize that the nature of a swarm is only apparently chaotic. Recognizing the swarms in our lives is an alternate right-brain way of looking at reality. Just consider the motion of these externals: food, molecular molecules, breath exchange, the displacement of hair, skin, urine, feces, saliva, sensations, thoughts, perceptions and inferences. All these swarms have the qualities of the three gunas.

Consider the food we eat every day. It usually comes from many places that are far from where we eat. The parts are a swarm of food. Then after digestion we send out fecal matter which gets dissolved and swarms into the planet through many means. The same happens to what we drink.

The furniture in our houses is another example of a swarm. All of it comes from the earth in different locations and is manufactured into parts in many places until after processing, selecting and delivery it comes to our house.

A more subtle swarm is the swarm of knowledge we absorb as we grow up. Only a small part of it is from formal education processes, a swarm of swarms itself. Our perceptions are a continual swarm that we can't turn off. And then we have a swarm of pre-existing judgments' about parts of the swarm: like, dislike, fear, etc.

All of these swarms involve selective choices by others and by us. These choices provide feedback to the swarms; some of it is aggregated and some of it is based on individual choices. If, for example, everyone in a particular city stopped eating bananas, the swarm of bananas heading towards the city would soon avert to other destinations. If you are slow to learn to read, the education that was swarming towards you is changed to a different swarm.

At this point we have to consider the swarm of human beings that form the city. Very small towns, for example, don't get bananas delivered (the bananas don't swarm to their location.

In large cities, we have swarms of criminals entering the justice system. The swarm leaving the justice system goes to many different places. The justice system itself consists of many different swarms, mostly slow moving: elected judges, various clerks, many types of lawyers, guards and policemen, etc. If we changed the criminal laws, e.g. legalization of marijuana, the swarm changes its type and quantity of criminals.

Memories images and concepts, likes and dislikes, fears and desires, valid and invalid knowledge, sleep and thoughts exist as patterns or "swarms" in consciousness. These swarms are constantly mutating, changing, becoming active or dormant, entering awareness or going into unconsciousness. At the death of the body consciousness goes on with the developed swarms. The body itself exists as a "swarm." It is a basic form of "change," the gunas.

Seeing "swarms" is obviously not a verbal exercise. At best we could say that we are our swarms. They are all stimulus-response in nature and are at times active, resistive, or clear. They can be pleasurable or painful.

These swarms make up what we think of as the person's karma. There are similar swarms that make up what we think of as countries and their karma, even planets or cosmos have karma. Separate from any swarms is the knowing of the swarms. The swarms are what we observe. Observations exist as patterns in consciousness. The knower of the patterns is awareness. Knowing is not personal. It only seems that way because of memory or likes and dislikes that bring up feelings. The likes and dislikes could be reduced to a list. It's bringing up feelings that make it seem personal. And, that is all conditioning.

The observed is what is personal, and it is merely a part of nature: swarms of gunic properties.

APPENDIX FIVE:
EXPERIENCE AND KNOWLEDGE OF THE "NOW"

1. We need to use a special language to talk or think about this subject because of the built in biases of language that are not readily understood. Among other problems is using the notions of "I," "me," "mine," "you," and "yours."

2. This is an issue because experience actually occurs immediately in the "now" without the involvement of memory; and language is unable to describe any experience adequately, let alone something not very well understood. What we experience are visual patterns, sound tones and physical sensations.

3. Real knowing does not depend on or require language.

4. Sensory perceptions occur immediately in what appears to be a timeless interlude without history. Without memory, perceptions are not understood; we could not discuss experience, know how to walk, or even know motion, for instance.

5. Experience includes what our sensory organs perceive: the perceptions of: sight, sound, smell, taste and touch. All of these are actually part of touch or contact. We also experience thoughts, and are fooled by the notion that "we" are thinking these thoughts.

6. The body is a sensory organ of experience; this body has a head only by inference based on memory: feeling with hand, seeing others that have heads, etc.

7. Experience also includes the momentary feelings generated by the body without external contact and images that are not caused by visual contact."Thinking with language involves memory; language

and memory are notoriously inaccurate and inadequate descriptions of experience especially experience of the "immediate now."

8. The feelings generated by the body along with the movements generated, are often reactions from something in the environment (based on memory).

9. Without memory, motion would not be apparent; language would not make sense; knowledge of any kind would not be available; the opposites (up/down, big/small, good/bad, mine/yours, etc.) would not be known; we would not know the Theosophical Society.

10. Experience in the "now" consists of patterns that depend on objects and not-objects, or shapes and not shapes.

11. Consciousness is a description of something that is inferred from an experience of existence. It implies something or someone can be conscious of something else; this ability is called being conscious, and it requires having consciousness. Because we experience objects, we say experience exists, and the objects that are perceived exist; they are together referred to as reality, what we are, have been, or could be conscious of.

12. The experience of thought can be generated internally or externally. Internal thoughts can be put on external speaker, so to speak; this sometimes happens accidently: e.g. thinking out loud.

13. When something "happens" in our experience, a reaction occurs. Avoiding a reaction is also a reaction. Reactions are not done consciously; they are spontaneous. They are not directed by language. They are not known until after the fact. Choices are actions.

APPENDIX SIX:
GROWTH:

APPLES	HUMAN BEINGS
Seed	Sperms
Conditions	Conditions: Womb, Eggs
Sprout	Fertilization
Sun, Moon	Conditions
Nourishment	Nourishment
Conditions	Conditions
Seasons	Seasons
Trees	
Conditions	
Flower	
Bees	
Pollination	
Baby Apple	Birth, Childhood, School,
Nourishment	Work
Conditions, Sun, Moon, Worms, Birds, Wind	Conditions
Maturity	Marriage
Falls	
Bugs, Birds, Worms	Sickness
Decay, Fermentation	Old Age, Sickness, Death
Returns to Earth	Returns to Earth
Sprouts	Born Again

When we see an apple we can infer its entire life; when we see a human being we can also infer its entire life. Human beings interpret their lives, but do not usually see the "suffering" that is inevitable throughout life.

APPENDIX SEVEN:
MIND MAPS:

The mind remember many important details about life that are, essentially, non-verbal. One of these non-verbal categories is maps. There are not only individual maps, but they are indexed with maps of maps. When we are in a conversation with a group, our maps of facial, postural and vocal inflections are in constant use and referred to automatically. Other typical maps are:

- Basic: names and forms; streets that you have lived and traveled on; stores that you know; faces that you know/knew; facial expressions: e.g. parental approval/disapproval

- Experiences: upsets (survival items); avoidances (things you don't like, don't want to repeat, etc.); attractions (things/people/experiences you like/dislike); things that you have learned (e.g. driving a car, riding a bike, engineering, trainings, arithmetic, how to find your way around the maps etc.); how to go to sleep; knowing languages; concepts;

- Egoism (a map that can pull up any of the above maps, consciously or unconsciously)

- Ignorance: valid maps that most of us don't have access to in our repertoire e.g. maps of "higher meditative experiences,"

- Maps can be created. This is critical after retirement when we need to redefine our working self to maintain our usefulness. There is a category of similar maps that can be described as maps of "being." In addition to the list in appendix three there are some other examples of how/what to be:

  o Responsible

  o Good

- o Bad

- o Complete (Don't leave a mess: home, work, car, garage, etc.)

- o Conscious (study/learn about: upsets, desires, fears, drugs, alcohol)

- o On purpose (sex, invitations, work)

- o Satisfied...Results

- o Diligent (keep on going, work for the good)

- Maps exist on the screen of consciousness where they are viewed by pure awareness. They become stronger the more they are used; they often trigger thoughts and feelings; they are necessarily not conscious because of the complexity of what they are doing. . Just walking is a complex operation, by itself. Think of talking and holding a conversation while watching others expressions; driving a car while texting; operating a computer. ...

APPENDIX EIGHT:
THE GUNAS:

The three gunas are discussed in most books on yoga. From my viewpoint, the early books didn't include much in the way of an explanation. A lot of the information on yoga was probably transmitted from the teacher to the student, verbally. Now, after a few years of being involved in the theosophical Advaita Vedanta Study Group, I seem to "know" more about the gunas than what was put in books. I don't see any reason not to describe what I know. First, another chart for review:

Raja	Tomas	Sattva	Comments
Active	Inactive	Intelligence	There are many descriptions.
Cause of action	Opposes action	Describes action	These descriptions are a little different.
Moving	Resists motion	Describes motion	
Alertness	Dullness	Conceptualizes	
Becomes conscious	Becomes unconscious		
Wakeful	Sleeps	Knows	
		Right knowledge	
Justifies action	Justifies inactivity	Explains anything	

Motion	Inertia	Light	
		Understanding	
Motion	Mass	Luminosity	
Impermanence	Solidity	Transparency	
Activating	Restraining	Illuminating	
Driven	Dullness	Awake	

These gunas are never separate. They are always in every part of nature, including human beings, corporations, and even nations, planets and the universe. When we realize that we are not "the thinker" then we can give up being obsessed with thought. Who we are as consciousness, can act "on purpose" where that can be creating our interpretations of events with thoughts while we operate one of the gunas (satva). Knowing that we are consciousness, which everything else is made of, gives us insight into what is needed in any given situation. Hint: it is not what will bring us comfort.

APPENDIX NINE:
JANA:

Classical Advaita Vedanta emphasizes the path of Jnana Yoga, a progression of study and training to attain liberation. It consists of four stages.

1. **Stage one:** The four fold discipline:

   a. This is the ability to correctly discriminate between an/the **eternal** substance (*Brahman*/god/consciousness) and substances that are of **transitory** existence.

   b. This is the renunciation of enjoyments of objects in this world and other worlds like heaven or better jobs or a better wife, etc.

   c. Develop the six fold qualities,

      1. Control the "I-Maker in the mind.

      2. Control the external sense organs from the pursuit of objects other than "consciousness."

      3. Give up the scriptural injunctions.

      4. Tolerate the " heat" that comes from suffering caused by internal forces like disease; the physical forces like earthquakes; and the karmic forces like friends and family.

      5. Keep faith in realized teachers and in the Vedas.

      6. Concentrate the mind on God and Guru.

   d. This is the firm conviction that the nature of the world is misery resulting in an intense longing for liberation.

2. **Stage Two:** Listen to the teachings of the sages on the **Upanishads** and **Advaita Vedanta**, and studying the Vedantic texts,

such as the **Brahma Sutras**. In this stage the student learns about the reality of <u>Brahman</u> and the identity of atman;

3. **Stage Three:** Reflect on the teachings.

4. **Stage four:** Meditate on the truth "that art Thou" or you are pure consciousness, Brahma. Think about what your consciousness is, for example, it accepts any thought or perception without resistance. The mind, on the other hand, resists many ideas, etc.

The question of no-origination or non-creation is argued often, but is the accepted doctrine of Guadapada: origination and cessation are unreal. Buddhist writers often indicate that since there are no essences in factors, change or creation is possible. Eternal, impersonal, unborn consciousness Absolute is Brahman, the one without a second; it is also identical with the individual Self of each of us.

The Absolute does not change; it is not subject to time or limitations; it is not born and it does not die.

To succeed with Jnana consider the following topics:

- Right view: know that the mind is wild; we will never be able to tame it totally.

- Right intention: keep a good heart.

- Right effort; train like you are getting ready for the Olympics.

- Right mindfulness: quiet down and pay attention.

- Right concentration: keep a focused mind.

APPENDIX TEN:
STOPPING THOUGHTS:

1. Count the out breath, going from one to four and then starting over.

2. If you lose count start over.

3. Do this for ten minutes at a time, a few times a day.

4. After practicing for a few days start to pay attention to the space between counting. Is it empty? Is there a slight sound associated with the emptiness? Are there body sensations observable? Can the space be expanded?

APPENDIX ELEVEN:
CAUSE AND EFFECT:

1. Much of life follows conditioning and conflicts between different operators.

2. Choosing actions based on commitment or training with the potential to change the direction of life, but it's always more of the same drama.

3. Any direction is still empty and meaningless, which leaves life open to interpretation: like/dislike/neutral, etc.

4. The universe started with a slight vibration of pure consciousness, without a purpose.

5. At the ordinary level of observation life is full of suffering.

6. At a higher level, life is an interesting drama.

7. At the highest level, life is God acting on God, creating the appearance of motion. The Self is God but not the usual image.

8. Creation is possible because this existence is empty and meaningless: we bring the meaning and interpretation to existence. Creation does not bring up anything new. What results from an apparent cause is just part of a continuous connected reality, as measured by time. Absolute consciousness does not change in any way.

9. We can only be the immediate cause of any action, e.g. lifting your right arm. We can do this if we are paying attention to the instruction, but we must first understand the language that we have been taught (conditioning). We also must have a right arm. Obviously we could have lost it in our history. Also, you must get the idea first or it would be a random motion. And, ideas are in the domain

of the mind or the gunas. We are not the mind. Thinking or acting "on purpose" is possible, but rare.

10. Normally we follow our inclinations and habits. This is necessary because we could not walk if we didn't have habits. What is needed is to discriminate between our normal stimulus-response activity and what is not stimulus-response. This is extraordinarily difficult. We have very strong repeating emotions, as well as what we like and usually do and what we don't like and how we usually don't do. In order to come to grips with this to any extent yoga practices are necessary or some extraordinary commitments in life. It's almost inevitable that some sleep will have to be sacrificed.

11. When we make a significant commitment we expect some creativity to manifest. Raising an arm is not usually a significant commitment. Deciding to get a college education is significant for most of us. Using that education goes even further. The commitments we make can change the world. Using language is only a method to involve the mind.

12. Any effect has an instrumental and a material cause. A table requires a carpenter and wood. The material cause is lost in the history of the universe, Brahma or God. The effect is the same as the cause; the table is still made of wood. The cause is different from the effect; the carpenter is different from the table.

13. The world is not different from Brahman, but Brahman is different from the world. The existence of forms is dependent on Brahman as the material and instrumental cause.

14. When considering cause and effect we can analyze four levels:

    a. The highest level is pure awareness that pervades all reality. Technically it is not a level, but it remains independent and untouched by existence. It is the ultimate knower.

    b. The absolute level of existence, pure consciousness is required for the lower two levels to exist.

c. The empirical level is existence on the level of the senses.

d. The conceptual level includes language, social agreements and the imagination that we use to live our lives.

APPENDIX TWELVE: CONDITIONING:

1. We are all conditioned from birth and childhood; most of us don't know it, and have never thought about it.

2. The forms of our conditioning are complex. Consider walking, for example: it's a conditioned habit that we learned at a young age and improved as we grew up. It's like driving a car; we need the conditioned responses because we are unable to react quickly enough for the circumstances that come up. Conditioning is not a negative effect. We need conditioning in life.

3. Not knowing that we are conditioned is a problem: we automatically react to circumstances to avoid things we don't like or don't want and try to obtain things we like or want. Eventually we are left with automatic response patterns that are no longer visible to us. We just act the way we always act and get the results we always get.

4. This becomes a problem when we are adults using the desires of a child and are unhappy with the results of our actions. Then we look for help of various types:

    • Diets

    • Marital counseling

    • Exercise programs

    • Yoga regimes

    • Budget development

    • Relationships

- Financial management programs
- Health tips

5. As the Sufis say-if you don't know that you are in jail, you can't break out of jail. We are in an emotional/mental jail that is called the "ego." Beyond that is our inability to see reality as it exists. We, in effect, have blinders on.

6. All of existence is conditioned; this is the kind of world we live in. In a sense most of the people we know are technically "insane." They keep doing the same things and expect different results.

7. Some conditioning is so ingrained that it apparently cannot be overcome in this life, other than for short specific periods using strong commitments. These include:

   o Depression

   o Anxiety

   o Many other mental illnesses

8. Often someone gets into some form of meditation/yoga and feels a touch of bliss and decides that this will work for their depression or anxiety. Sometimes it does; other times it doesn't. When medicine will help; take it.

APPENDIX THIRTEEN:
HATHA YOGA:

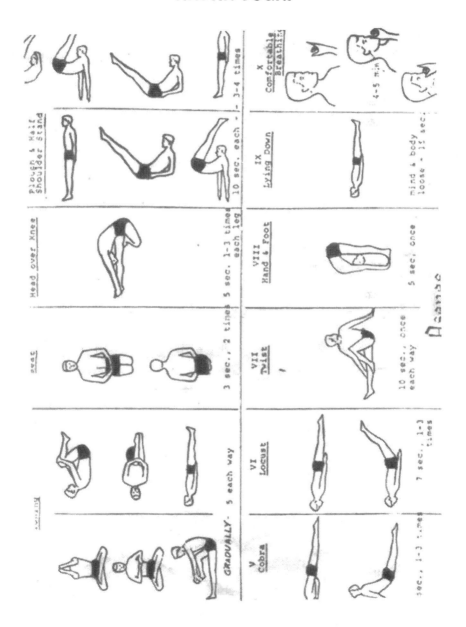

The practice of hatha yoga seems, at first, to be less esoteric than meditation exercises. The significance of massage, stretching, balancing and breathing exercises relate directly to the many stresses that condition us as we grow and develop. As they are relieved, our meditation practice grows; we get insight into our conditioning.

APPENDIX FOURTEEN: GLOSSARY

- Absolute existence is pure consciousness

- Atman is Sanskrit term for the higher Self, consciousness.

- Awareness underlies all our perceptions.

- Bondage is when we, unknowingly are stuck in our conditioning.

- Brahman is a Sanskrit term for everything/nothing; it's qualities are Eternal Bliss Consciousness

- Commitment is a promise made our self to accomplish a goal in life.

- Consciousness is boundless and timeless.

- Creation does not happen; all we have is continual change as expressed by consciousness.

- Dream objects are real from the point-of-view of the mind.

- Emptiness of Inherent Existence/no essence is a common Buddhist insight into existence. It relates to the idea that all this is empty and meaningless; we bring meaning to our lives.

- God has many names in language. Here it is synonymous with Brahma, consciousness and the Self.

- Egoism is the accumulation of kleshas. Its expression is always changing.

- Experience is knowledge that is different from conceptual. It combines consciousness with reality. There is no boundary between experience and the observing consciousness.

- Freedom is when we can transcend conditioning.

- Freedom is having the ability to understand conditioning and being able to make promises that you can always keep in spite of conditioning.

- Free will occurs when we transcend our conditioning.

- Gunas are three qualities that are in every form of existence.

- Constituents of Human Beings

- Kleshas are the barriers to "enlightenment:" survival, avoidance, attraction, egoism and ignorance of the situation.

- Knowing without subject and object: the perceiver is the perceived.

- Knowledge of existence depends on memory and successive moments of "now."

- The known is what is perceived. All we know are our perceptions floating in consciousness.

- Life is what we go through between birth and death. It is most pronounced when we make major changes in our situations.

- Love is ineffable. We always misunderstand what it means, usually settling for some form of attraction. A Sufi saying, as I remember, is when you don't know who someone is you love them, when you do know who someone is you are them.

- Stages of dying: denial, anger, bargaining, depression, acceptance

- Mahavakyas are four sayings of the sages:
    o Consciousness is Brahman (God)
    o I am Brahman
    o That thou art (you are God)
    o This Atman is Brahman (this self is God)

- The manifold universe is one single connected reality, one great being; it is pure consciousness, Brahman or God. It holds all the forms of existence and non-existence.

- Nonduality refers to the interconnected reality of all things

- Reality: the true reality is Brahman, which is not the same as the perceived reality.

- Relinquishment is giving up expectations of results from action, e.g. some reward for doing good, or punishment for doing bad, etc.

- Renunciation is giving up desires, e.g. money, food, sex, etc.

- Self/self-The true self is pure consciousness, and is designated by "Self."

- Self is not found when we look. There is nothing that meets our idea of an independent self; there is only consciousness.

- Space is what lets us distinguish objects.

- Time is a result or expression of consciousness. It lets us distinguish motion.

- Ultimate reality is the absolute, pure consciousness. Pure awareness is "higher" but is not part of existence; it is the ultimate knower.

Coming next: *The Vedanta Sutras:* an Inquiry into the Nature of God.

28251191R00153

Made in the USA
Charleston, SC
06 April 2014